HEALING UNDER TROPICAL SKIES

By Evelyn Whitell

AUTHOR OF

*Shekinah; The Silence; The Christmas Guest;
The Woman Healer; A California Poppy;
Healing Silences; Extraordinary Mary;
The Arms of Love and Wings of Faith;
Lovingly in the Hands of The Father;
The 23rd Psalm in Silence*

DeVorss & Co., *Publishers*
843 SOUTH GRAND AVENUE
LOS ANGELES, CALIFORNIA

.

*Printed in the United States of America by
DeVorss & Co., 843 S. Grand Ave.,
Los Angeles, California*

CONTENTS

Healing Under Tropical Skies

CHAPTER I

ALOHA!

A land where everyone gets well! Arthur Seaton repeated these words as he sat under the giant palm tree, watching with tired interest the surf-board riders at Waikiki. He felt like a lost soul amidst this brilliant scene of light and color. He watched the strong young Hawaiians race with their canoes, dive from the highest points into the waves or standing erect on their surfboards, riding towards the shore, like ships swept homeward by a rapid wind.

A land where everyone gets well! It was the belief in this which had brought him across the water just two weeks before. He remembered how the physician had told him that the cause of his continual sickness was only in the mind, and how, if he mixed with the vibrant youth of the day, lived in a land of sunshine and flowers, he would become as strong as an average man of his age. It was hard at first to get such a belief into a subconscious mind, which for twenty-five years had been registering a different story.

His early training had been against him. His parents, he was constantly reminded, had passed with lung trouble, and the same fatality had been held over him since birth. The maiden aunt who had adopted him with his fortune, had raised him on cod-liver oil and cough drops, kept him indoors over the winter and had his tutor in the home.

Arthur loved books and study. He came of a race of ministers and teachers. He lived in the mental world, and as many mothers were fond of quoting to their negligent sons and daughters, he knew the Bible from cover to cover. He believed as his parents and grandparents had believed, swallowed their idea of God, and though his religion gave him little comfort, clung to it with that deep sincerity which comes of a conscientious ancestry.

The sudden passing away of his maiden aunt, roused him from a dream of twenty-five years. It came with a shock and an intense surprise, because Aunt Amy had been to him like a fixture. She had spoken many times of the other world, but never in connection with herself. It had been her consolation to him when his cough was unusually bad, that God did not let suffering go on forever, but had prepared a place of rest. He had seen himself in that oasis a thousand times, but never placed Aunt Amy anywhere except amidst her church work and with her knitting by the fire-side.

"What will that delicate nephew do, now poor Miss Seaton has gone on?" was the question asked on all sides. Arthur was wondering too. He had acted so little independently that the responsibility of being thrown upon his own resources was appalling. It was then that his physician had spoken to him of the trip to the Hawaiian Islands, and at the words "A land where everyone gets well," he had felt a desire to see beyond the place where he was living. Life had become suddenly interesting to him, and he had found himself repeating again and again, the doctor's words—"a land where everyone gets well."

He had continued to think of this as he lay in the darkness of his room at night. It was the first throb of hope for his future that he had ever felt. He had only a vague idea of the islands of which the doctor had spoken. He had associated them mostly with a race of heathen which his aunt had told him it was her prayer that he might go forth some day to convert. Closing his eyes for a moment, overcome by the immensity of taking such a trip alone, possible he touched in consciousness the shores of that other world. He never knew whether he dreamed it, but in the afterwards he recalled many times that quick flash out of the nothingness of darkness, the picture of a shore beaten by shining waves, skies of a brilliant blue, giant palms and blossoms through which the smiling face of a flower crowned woman looked and waved her hands in welcome.

"A land where everyone gets well." He had made up his mind to try it and he dared not voice the beautiful hope, but it registered in his subconscious mind.

* * *

The voyage was what he had built into it. No sooner had he stepped on deck, when the first thing he heard was a conversation of a man with his wife. "Now my dear," he was saying, "you are certain to be sick, most people are on this trip and you are a poor sailor. It would be better for you to go down to your stateroom, lie on your back and have all your meals brought down to you."

Arthur had glanced for a moment at this strong, healthy looking woman, and had wondered ironically if the husband had anything up his sleeve that he desired to keep his wife in the state-room while he was on deck. Nevertheless, in his nervous condition the fear got him

and the voyage was one of misery and sickness. He kept
in his room until the last day, when weak and desperately
ill, he stepped on deck realizing that he had put between
himself and home, a barrier that he would never be able
to cross.

The cry that Honolulu was in sight, had brought all
the people to the vessel's edge. He was glad in the great
excitement of getting ashore, no one had seemed to
notice his condition.

The Matsonia was gliding over the waters, golden
with the morning sunrise, like a happy seagull sailing
easily for home. Lights of rose and amber struck her
sides like flags of victory to herald her approach. Out
of the shining blue of the sky, rain, delicate as dew, was
falling, and away over Diamond Head, a rainbow
sparkling like jewels wrote her cheerful 'Aloha' in the
brightest colors.

Everyone was pressing to the vessel's edge. Handsome
American girls and big-eyed laughing Hawaiians, tiny
Japanese mothers holding up smiling black-haired babies;
men, women and children straining their necks and eyes
to see in the distant crowd upon the landing stage, someone they loved awaiting them with leis.

He had found himself jostled into the midst of the
happy throng. Their great vibration of joy and expectant
love, the warmth of their throbbing hearts, the kisses
ready on their lips, their arms vibrating to embrace their
loved ones, threw out an energy on every side, which had
warmed his starved body with a warmth no sunshine
could have given. It had brought a sudden strength
and vitality which made him forget his weakness and
straighten his bent frame.

The boat was drifting nearer. Shouts of recognition
filled the air, mingling their joy with the burst of music

which came with sudden and surprising sweetness from the great Hawaiian band; music that rang out on it's tender notes the welcome of the Islands, a welcome so full of joy and beauty that it roused emotion almost to the joy of tears.

He had sung with the happy people, he who had never sung beyond the humming of a hymn. It seemed impossible to believe as he walked down the gangway and saw the leis around every neck, that there was not some-one there to welcome him. The soulful rapture had continued to stir within him while the taxi went over the ground, through hedges made brilliant by pink and red hibiscus, where the golden shower trees tossed their flaming colors against the shining blue of the sky, under the tall shelter of the majestic white trunked palms, to the modern hotel, so like the surroundings by which he had been associated, that the damp had begun to settle once more on his soul, especially when the clerk looked at his name and said, "Oh, yes, your lawyer wrote to us. He made your reservation. It's Mr. Seaton, the invalid, is it not?"

The invalid! In those moments of contagious joy, he had forgotten that he ever was one. Yes, of course he was an invalid. He felt it far more strongly when he went down to the beach at Waikiki. Men and women of all ages sporting with the shining tide; children like rain drenched flowers, playing their games of catching with the waves—and he alone a stranger on the beach, unable to take part in any of their fun. He longed, as he had never longed, for a strong body, to be able to do what other men could do.

A land where everyone gets well! He sat now thinking over these words. That was not so with him, he sat here weak and ill. He made up his mind that it was of no use remaining on the beach. Slowly he returned to the hotel. Parties of men and women playing bridge under the cool air fan, looked pityingly towards him, as he walked into the lounge, keeping as far away as he could from the open doors. One or two of the prettiest girls, induced by a sympathetic man, who noticed his forlorn condition, invited him to join them in the games, but because he had been raised in a home where such things were forbidden, he answered curtly enough, so they bothered him no more, and finding nothing with which to amuse himself, he went up to his room.

Why, he asked himself, was he so different from these strange human beings; none of them natives, most of them from the land where he had lived; some probably from his own State, and yet so far removed from him. At night he could not sleep. The hotel was noisy, the merry laughter of the pleasure makers came through his open windows, mixed with the voices of lovers singing "The moon, Ah me, the moon at Waikiki," or the sound of the ukulele in the Aloha, or the trade wind whipping through the palms.

"I am not used to this kind of life," he told the doctor, who came in answer to his call. "Where I lived there was silence and rest, but here, everyone seems full of nervous energy. There is no time for quiet or peace. I want to read and study, but to do that I have to remain in my room where it is hot and close, and if I put on the air fan, it gives me a cold."

"Have you always been like this?" asked the dotcor, trying to repress a smile.

"More or less, yes," answered Arthur, "but I was told this was a land where everyone got well, and I came out here full of hope."

"So you want a place where you can be quiet? You have not reached it in Honolulu, this bright little town where everyone is like an uncorked bottle of champagne, as soon as they touch the glories of Waikiki, but if you want quiet and silence for study, (though I cannot see why anyone should want to bury his nose in a book when there is so much to see outside of one) then, I'll tell you what to do—go to another island. There's a spot loved by the Hawaiians, a spot where the old natives dwell. At a certain part of the beach in that little nest of love, they say it is impossible to be sick. If you want silence, if you want a patch of Heaven here on earth, a garden of Eden in which no serpent dwells, you'll find it on that little island standing by itself, as if it had been broken off from one of the bigger islands or just dropped out of the sky. The boats which carry the sightseers to other parts, never touch it. No tourist has stamped his name on its beautiful trees. It is sacred to the natives, and when they leave it for the city, they go back again in no time. Some speak our language well, and some can't understand it. The men spend their time in their fishing boats; the women bringing up their babies. You will find them kind and helpful, interesting in the way they live. If they get word of your arrival, they will come out in their canoes to pick you up from the big boat. There is no other way to get there. In times past, the kings would reach each island through a passage underground, but of those we know nothing now, for they died with their secrets, and if the old native knows them still, he will not give them away. Go to Kuhali, and there you'll find what a nature like yours craves. The beach will be just like your own."

But Arthur shook his head. The thought of the waves and the state-room in which he had spent six days of agony in crossing from the coast, brought the color of sea-sickness to his face.

"I don't think anything would help me," he said weakly. "My father tried all things—my mother too, but they both passed with the same trouble."

The doctor spoke strongly and emphatically. "Come, man," he said, "you're not your father nor your mother, so you need not blame them for your present condition. We are too fond of blaming our weak spots on another. Because my great grandfather died in the workhouse is the very reason why I am not going to die there. We learn by the mistakes of others, but if we are going to copy their mistakes, we would make a funny muddle of our lives. You go to Kuhali, and if you don't get better when three weeks have passed, I'll give up my profession."

"Unfortunately that wouldn't help me," said Arthur. "If I could reach this place by land, I would go willingly —but, water—"

"Yes, of course you fear the water. I guess they wrapped you up too much in a blanket, instead of throwing you up in one. The trouble with you is, you think of nothing but your precious body."

"Oh, no!" cried Arthur, in a voice of an ancestry of ministers. "I think about my soul."

"Then think about your soul, and get away from your body," answered the doctor, as he went from the room.

The words struck home. The doctor was right. He must think of his soul. He had not dwelt on that lately, and how did he know but what his soul might soon be required of him. He would go to the next island and give that little place a chance. In solitude he would have time for prayer and reading his Bible, so that if the end should come, it might be peaceful as the end of his ancestors had been.

Deep in his heart he wanted to live, but he wanted to live and be well. He was tired of dragging around a weak and ailing body. He wanted to be strong as the men who rode the surf-boards. It might come—but now he must think of his soul.

CHAPTER II

SAILING INTO THE ISLAND OF HEALTH

He did not feel the roughness of the passage to Maui. He was lying alone in his state-room. The waves hit hard on the vessel and more than once thundered the deck. He was surprised when the steward brought him his supper, to hear that some of the people were sick. He was conscious of a certain victory when he stepped out on deck and looked at the heaving water, over which he had gained dominion.

The wind blew strong and cold. They were passing the twinkling lights of an island. "That's Molokai," said one of the men who sat beside him. "If you're a stranger you may not know the points of interest. The leper islands are always of interest to me. I visited one once. I made myself do it because I had a friend there. It was a hard thing for me to do, but I thought of Robert Louis Stephenson, how he said his greatest horror in life was the horror of the horrible, but he overcame that because compassion was aroused in his soul when he once found out the loneliness of those outcasts. On the island I visited, there was a beautiful case of love and devotion, which was to me the brightest spot in its history. It was the case of a man with very small symptoms of the disease. He was cured by the oil treatments they are giving, but before he was cured he had fallen in love with one of the women. Strange for a man to fall in love with a leper—but such was the case."

"Sympathy," suggested Arthur, with his eyes still fixed on the lights of the island, now fading away like stars in the mist.

"Sympathy? No! One looks for that in a woman, but it is a mighty rare jewel to find in a man. It was a case of real love but not at first sight. He was one of the most prosperous men of his day, the pet of society, a man of the world. He was just on the verge of marrying a beautiful woman, but suddenly where fortune's wheel had worked in his favor, she swung in the other direction, and all was gone in a night. Then his so-called friends began to walk on the other side of the street. The girl he was to have married, told him in a few violet-scented words, that it would now be impossible for her to consider it, and on top of all this he was found to have symptoms of the disease. He was brought to the Islands, and it was there he met this lonely, sad hearted woman. Her experience had been something like his own, but she seemed to forget it in cheering him. She was not a clever woman, and I do not suppose she was very good looking, but she gave him a love such as he had never known, and of course she grew slowly into his heart."

Arthur smiled somewhat sadly. "It's very romantic," responded the man. "It's strange, too, what tricks fortune can play. I never worry over her games any more than I worry when the sun goes back of a cloud, for I know that the moment she has dashed our ship on the rocks, she is just as likely to bring one in full sail round the corner, a far better ship than the one we have lost. It was just such a game she played with this man. After taking all out of his hands, she flung back her golden ball in his lap. All things came raining down in a moment. He was cured, as I say, by the oil treatments, and freedom's gate opened before him; and just on that very morning with the sudden rush in of good planets, he heard he had fallen sole heir to his uncle's estate. He was the owner of millions. No one rejoiced more than his little companion. She told him she had prayed all the time for his freedom. Women tell us they pray for some strange things, and it's hard for us selfish men to believe it, but I do honestly think that good little woman wished him the best, even if it meant sorrow for her.

"Of course, after the news of his riches were circulated, letters of congratulation came in on all sides; letters from those who had long since forgotten him. The girl he was to have married, wrote to own her mistake, and confess that her love had gone to no other. Do you think he went back to them? He made the woman who was a leper, believe he was going, just to test her love to the limit, but she stood it out to the end. Without a tear but a mighty big lump in her throat, she bid him good-bye. She would not go down to the boat and she didn't need to, because he never intended to go. He waited until night time, and then slipped around to her cottage. She was kneeling at prayer. She was praying for him. Not for him to come back, but that he might find his own, and be happy."

The man stopped a moment. Arthur was somewhat surprised to see he was wiping his eyes. The world is more quick to sympathize than we believe.

"And then?" he asked slowly.

"Why, then they married," he continued, growing suddenly practical. "Married, and lived on the Island. Do you think he would leave a woman like that? No, he had found love at last, and he would rather live with love in a leper settlement than in a world of society without it."

"That was a very unusual case," Arthur said.

"Yes, pretty unusual, because people are seeking for fortunes in our days and not seeking love."

Arthur smiled wearily. "I cannot give an opinion on that," he replied, "I never sought either."

"That's maybe your trouble," the stranger suggested. "Don't call it a virtue not to have loved, for unless we have love in our lives, we had better be dead—or we are dead, would be truer, for nothing can live without love, it would pine away like an unwanted plant in the cellar. Love, man, even if it breaks your heart. Love, even if your ideals are smashed in the loving; love, and if your life is only transformed by that love but a moment, you will have touched the robes of glory such as not all the cold dollars of the world could buy."

" I was never very interested in women," Arthur coolly responded.

The man laughed heartily. "Oh, love does not necessarily mean a woman," he answered, "though that's the love we generally crave. But love something, and however small may be the object of your love, it will light a spark in your world which will save you from utter desolation."

"I love my God," said Arthur, with an effort.

His companion grew suddenly silent. He had lifted his eyes to the blackness of the sky, made brilliant by millions of glittering stars. Then, he looked down to the man by his side and fixed his gaze earnestly on him. The light from the window of one of the staterooms, fell over his face, white, miserable and drawn by years of sickness. Was he the expression in body and mind of one who loved even the smallest things in nature, the tiniest microbe, of the Great Cause of All?" Where was the vibrant atmosphere, the radiant life, the luminance and power? Without connecting with its object, love would be an impossibility. If this man truly loved his God, he must have divine connection, yet, what had this connection brought him?

"I am not what the world calls religious," he said slowly. I know creation has a cause and that cause manifests in everything. I can see it as much in those big dashing waves, as I can in that crescent moon, but I haven't got the understanding of that Cause, and to love a thing we have to understand it. If you have got that understanding strong enough to love it, then you're a lucky man, for love connected with the Cause of all, should bring you all things."

"A lucky man! trying to hold thoughts for the salvation of his soul, he sat out shivering in the deck. Where was his luck?" he questioned.

A troupe of happy laughing girls and boys, glorying in wind and waves and starlit skies, came rushing past him. "Their sea-sickness didn't bother them much," said the gentleman as he watched them race the deck. "You can't keep life and health like that tied down."

"It must be wonderful to have such energy," Arthur replied. "I never had it, even as a boy. They told me I would get well if I came to this island, and I came with a great hope in my heart."

"And so you will get well, if you get the spirit expressed here, the joy of the native with his surf-board; the delight of the flower crowned maidens at Waikiki—if you get into the waves and live like a native."

"I have more to do with my life than to waste it like that," interrupted Arthur.

"What?"

He paused—but in the silence that followed the question, he was thinking.

"What?" asked the man again. "What are you doing with your life? It's no business of mine, but as a student of human nature, I am interested."

"I read and I contemplate."

"And then?"

"I have not been able to do much yet, my health has prevented it."

"Then, why not turn all your study to your health? Emerson has said 'A sick man is a villain,' and I will tell you that there is nothing in the world that makes a man so cranky and miserable as when he is dragging around an ailing body."

"I quite agree with you," Arthur responded, "but to me it seems impossible to get well. I have tried all things and coming here was a last resource."

"Yet you are connected with the Cause that built the worlds. "You say you love that Cause—surely your love must gain response in the eternal energy of Love."

A faint flush crept to Arthur's cheeks. "You don't believe as I do," he said, "and I don't often talk on religion."

"Nor I," replied the man. "I don't, because I don't know much about it. I have my own ideas of things, and I guess I have the license to express them. I said I knew there was a Cause for this creation, the Cause that you call God, but which of us have found Him? We get glimpses of His glory on a night like this. We have moments of it on the mountain heights, moments of great emotional rapture, which make the world look very cold when we step out of it—but if the Force of all of our love were concentrated on His Power, love being the greatest magnet that there is, we should become like gods ourselves. How could man fail, connected with that mighty dynamo? How could he draw into his life the sorrows of the world, since sorrow has no part in that divine connection? How could he be weak and sick when the architect has no flaw? How could he die, since eternal energy is deathless? His life would become like a strong river, drawing always from a never ending source."

He walked away as he spoke, and Arthur was glad to see him go. Somehow this conversation made him nervous. He leaned back in his deck chair, watching the dancing lights upon the water, and longing that the trip might end.

Chapter III

LILINOE

When Arthur had been three days in Hona he found himself gradually gaining strength. He had taken a little cottage in sight of the water and employed a Chinaman for cook and housekeeper.

Yee Kui was a man past middle life, given to sucking a pipe rather than smoking, and thinking more than he expressed. It was this last virtue which pleased Arthur, who was worn out by the constant babel of tongues which clashed over nothing in the lobby of the hotel.

Yee Kui was kind and thoughtful for his master, ministering to his smallest needs, but asking no question, understanding his wants, more by intuition than by words.

He began to enjoy his life of freedom, spending his time out of doors and finding his meals ready at whatever hour he returned. Sometimes he questioned how the silent footed little Chinaman could provide such unexpected delicacies which had the relish he had always craved. It amused him that he should really feel hungry, and yet Yee Kui never provided too much nor too little, but smiled at the empty plates, with a smile so quaint and kindly that it made one forget that his mouth was toothless.

The lights went out early all over the Island, but Yee Kui always had candles provided. As he placed them by the bedside, he would make his friendly bow with the word spoken slowly, "Master sleepee verree well."

Arthur was glad he said it without the hope. He like the strength of the affirmation, "Sleepee verree well."

And he did sleep. He slept better than he had ever done in his life. He had never really slept with comfort. As a child he was disturbed by nervous fears, nightmares and dreams, and had more than once walked in his sleep. He remembered how his aunt, fearing that he might walk out of doors on some of these somnambulistic rambles, had had him tied in bed. How he had screamed in vain for his release and finally broken one of his teeth in trying to bite through the rope—but he was suddenly knowing what it was to sleep, and sleep easily.

On the third morning he did not awaken until nearly daybreak. The bright light of the stars was softening with the coming dawn. He did not know that he had ever seen a sunrise. A feeling of interest awoke in his heart, an interest which gave him a sudden grip of life. He would go out and watch for the sun to rise; how surprised Yee Kui would be if he got up ahead of him, and was out of doors before he had time to prepare his breakfast. A touch of fun almost akin to a school boy's, made him enjoy the anticipation of the picture. It cost him a little effort to dress without assistance, but he forgot everything in his eagerness to steal this march on Yee Kui.

But those who got up ahead of the Chinaman would have to say up all night. Yee Kui's little watchman, of whom nobody knew but himself, because he lived in the finest crevice of his ear, was there at all hours with his bell, and had given him the morning call before Arthur was out of bed. The tray with the hot coffee and toast met him at the door, and asking no question, Yee Kui placed it on the table and shuffled away, a smile on his face broadening at his master's amazement.

"Upon my word, Yee Kui, if you aren't the limit," said Arthur. "I was going to have the surprise on you, but you got it on me."

He drank the coffee and went on his way rejoicing in the freedom of not being asked where or why, or even the hour when he would return.

Nature came forward to meet him in all the grandeur of her morning glory. The air was damp with the heavy moisture of the night and the salty spray of the sea. A soft primrose light, deepening into gold around the throne of the rising sun, reflected on the glittering sand. A sea bird shining white against the green of Pali-Ulis heights dropped suddenly downwards and joined her companions in their morning sail across the glittering waves.

Arthur walked slowly under the cocoanut trees and down to where the pink flowered vine trained over the stones to meet the sea.

A dark-skinned, smiling native with a lei of red hibiscus twisted about his straw hat called out a cheerful "Aloha" as he pulled his bright canoe from among the others and pushing it into the billows, paddled away from the shore.

Arthur liked this spirit of greeting, though he had yet to learn the beautiful meaning of the beautiful word. He felt glad to be treated like a rational being and not always looked upon as an invalid.

The beach was very still and restful; the calm, clear air, so full of scents carried from hidden shrubs and mountain flowers, scarcely disturbed the gentle movement of the waves. A peace like he had never known stole over him. It seemed as though a cool and sympathetic hand had suddenly been laid upon his heart; as if a calm and gentle voice demanded every nerve to be at rest. He relaxed in its security like a child long frightened by shadows would relax in the protection of its mother's arms. He did not want to break this beautiful charm; he stayed out all morning, basking in it, feeling happy in the knowledge that Yee Kui would not seek for him, nor even question if he did not return at any stated hour. It was very convenient to live with someone who did not follow him with an anxious mind, nor wonder where he was. Better, far better, than a hundred telephones was the magic understanding of this silent little Chinaman. He ventured to stay the afternoon; he did not feel hungry, and he knew his lack of hunger did not come from illness. He was getting a royal feast in the glory of the beautiful scene on which he looked. No one to bother him. The strong fishermen threw in their nets, but their energy did not tire him like the energy of the bathers at Waikiki.

Night was approaching. Where the great King of day had sunk to rest, the stars were scattered like jewels fallen from a crown of gold. Over the crimson path of light the heavy blinds of darkness were being drawn. Arthur was surprised to find he was almost drowsy; drowsy without using all the sense-numbing, suggestion-brewed remedies of the drug store and the doctor. He rolled his steamer rug into a ball, rested his head upon it, and gave way to this new sensation of sleep without drugs and thumping a pillow. How long he slept he did not know, but he was jerked suddenly into consciousness by the sound of a rock rolling from heights above and falling at a little distance. He strained his eyes in the darkness with difficulty recalling his whereabouts. By the light of a thousand stars he could dimly discern the giant outline of the cliff behind him. In front the waves of an invisible tide came washing inwards. He drew like a frightened child into the shelter of the protecting heights, as he felt the salt spray splash upon his face and hair. Stiff and cold, with aching limbs, he tried to find his way along the sand. He had congratulated himself on freedom; that no one interfered with his movements; but how much he longed now for a human voice, for some one's guiding hand. He was almost angry with Yee Kui for leaving him in such a plight. Each step he took seemed to bring him into denser darkness. He had no idea of his whereabouts except he knew he was close to the sea, sandwiched between the mighty waves and the giant cliffs.

All in a moment he stood still. The same sound which had awakened him came again. His surroundings were forgotten; fear took another note as he looked upwards. Far above on the perilous heights, where it seemed impossible for any human foot to reach, a light was moving like a falling star. His heart began to beat to suffocation. Every nerve of his body stood on end, yet fascinated, he watched the strange descending gleam, appearing, dying into darkness, then flashing forth again upon a lower point. Ghosts were not real to him. He had not, fortunately, been frightened like most children by ugly, untrue stories, but there was something horribly uncanny in that far off traveling light, especially when he realized that it was not unaccompanied, for he was positive in the black darkness he could trace the outline of a form. No human being could possibly scale such heights, he was certain. Yet the closer he fixed his eyes upon the cliff, the more sure he became that it was a human form. Watching it made him gain more courage; reason came to the foreground; the trance condition in which his sudden awakening had left him began to pass away. His brain grew clearer as he found his foothold on the earth. He was about to call when suddenly the light flashed close beside him. He heard the rustle of a garment. Someone had touched the ground as lightly as a bird, and almost as if on wings was gliding out of sight.

Now that he knew for certain that it was a human being he called out desperately and tried to follow in her tracks. She heard his voice and turned and flashed her light upon him. In its rays he saw a pair of large and startled eyes, the true type of Hawaiian face, unusually beautiful in the tenderness of its expression—hair crowned with flowers, and lips soft, sweet and lovable. Arthur could not tell why in that swift glance there should come to him something so familiar. Where had he seen that face before? It looked at him out of the mists of memory. One seemed as embarrassed as the other, but Arthur was the first to speak.

"Why are you out so late?" he asked, and then felt the absurdity of the question, for he did not even know the hour. Darkness fell early on the island, and anyway, what were this girl's affairs to him?

She laughed—the true, care-free Hawaiian laugh.

"Why, what about yourself?" she asked. "Aren't you out late as well?"

"I know, but I am a man," he answered, lamely.

"And I am a woman," she replied. "I guess I've got as good a reason to be out as you."

"But those rocks I saw you coming down—If you had slipped you would have dashed to pieces."

"And if you had fallen asleep and the waves come high enough to get you, it would have been all pau," she answered as she linked her arm in his with the great friendliness of the Hawaiian.

She was carrying something in her hand besides the flashlight. He was conscious by the sweet, delicious scent, that it was flowers. Surely there was a flora grand enough down here without her climbing those great heights. She did not give him time to question.

"You're from the coast," she said, with that rapidity which drifts the mind into another channel. "I never went there and I never want to go. This is my land. I love it, don't you?"

He answered, "Yes," not because of courtesy, but because he was growing more and more to realize that he did.

"They say they have lovely things where you come from, but they can't have grander things than we have here. People who come to us somehow do not look happy, but when they stay awhile, they never want to go away. They say it is like a fairy tale—our colors, flowers and rainbows. You will not want to leave when the time has come."

Would not he? It made him think. He was not looking to the future, but the question for the moment rose before him as he walked with her along the sand. Would it be possible that life to him might, after all, wear those bright robes she spoke of, and that the beauty of this land might sink so deeply into his whole being that it would hold him by its golden cord forever?

"Do you read fairy tales?" she asked.

"I cannot say I do," he answered. "I never read them even as a child. Real things of life appeal to me."

Her laugh broke out with merry sweetness. "If you had known our brownies and our menahunes, you wouldn't have been left out on the beach," she said. "They would have built a path right to your door and led you through it."

It did not interest him to hear these foolish superstitions of the Islands, yet he indulged her fancy for a moment.

"I suppose they built the path for you down from those heights you were descending?" he said.

"Heights do not bother me," she replied, "since I was born upon their summit."

They stopped that moment at the cottage. He had only been a few yards away, yet what a barrier the darkness formed.

"I never asked your name," she said. "Mine's Lilinoe; what's yours?"

He answered it was Mr. Seaton.

"But what's your given name? We don't have any Misters here. If we call people Mister we don't like them. I'd rather call you by your given name."

He drew in at the frank suggestion. How little he had heard that given name. Having no relatives to speak of, he was the only Mr. Seaton of his family. The servants in the home had called him "Master Seaton" in his childhood, changing the Master to Mister when he reached his teens. His tutor always honored him by "Mr. Seaton," His aunt spoke of him to everyone as "Mr. Seaton," and so rarely used his given name in front of others that it would sound foreign on another tongue.

She bent towards him suddenly and fastened something on his coat. The scent of it was rich and beautiful. Long years afterwards when in the heavy traffic of his strenuous life of service, through the golden doors of memory that scent would come wafting towards him, bearing him out for the moment to sun-kissed shores, and bringing him back rested and refreshed and stronger for the work he had to do.

The clock was striking twelve. He almost gasped. He had never been out so late. Where was the world in which he lived? It seemed to have vanished like the girl into the oblivion of the night. He was startled by a voice beside him. It was Yee Kui with his evening meal. He might have been acting the scene of the morning over again with another addition to the tray. . .

* * *

That night Arthur was wakeful but not with the restlessness of sickness. He had put the flower in water by his bedside. He had never had flowers in his room before. The doctor forbade them, and his aunt had not cared for the trouble they caused by the continual dropping of leaves on the tablecloth. This flower to him looked unusual; but did not most of the flowers of the Island look so? They seemed to have absorbed the colors of the rainbow, the sunsets and the wonderful dawns. He fell asleep looking on the brilliant red petals shining like lifeblood beneath the light of the flickering candle.

CHAPTER IV

THE LUAU

The fishermen had become interested in the man who sat on the beach. They looked on him at first much in the same way as the old natives must have looked on Captain Cook when he landed on the Island. So few things happened in that little out-of-the way Eden. The boats came in once a week and left next morning. The few passengers who arrived, seldom stayed longer than a day. The beauty of the scenery could not make up to the commercial man for lack of accommodation, for lights going out early, for rough uneven roads, and for the little interest taken in the salesman's goods. To have an outsider remain, was a treat, even though he sat all the time with rugs and shawls on the sand and seemed to do nothing but read.

Jack Oahu and his friend Iao Hapai, two of the strongest men of the island, were the first to make his acquaintance. They took him out in their canoes and tried to persuade him to go into the waves on a surf-board.

Arthur had great admiration for the strength of these immense fishermen, who drew in their nets with arms like iron—dived from the highest points—beat the roughest seas and could eat a raw fish from mouth to tail in a way that would make the average man shudder. They lived in a little hut by the water side—lived on poi and fish and sea moss. They knew every legend on the island, every old story handed down from age to age.

Their good nature, their willingness to serve, made them universal favorites. They had always the strong arm for their brother, and it was the lack of physical strength in the man from the coast that called forth their desire to help him. They never suggested he was sick—never talked to him of sickness—never presumed that he was in any way different from the rest of them. Arthur liked this—it lifted him from a world of which he was tired; unconsciously too, he was contacting the strength of these young fishermen as he watched them each day go into the waves with their nets. He was absorbing the great overflow of vitality thrown off in magnetic currents from their strong and powerful bodies.

It was Jack and Iao who induced him to go to the luau when he had been two weeks on the island. "We have a good time and we're all of us happy," said Jack by way of persuasion. "It's the feast that our fathers and mothers enjoyed before the white man set foot on the island. Be one with us and we won't feel you're a bird from another country."

Arthur hesitated before he accepted. He knew so little of the people and his solitude was to him more inviting than company. Jack's good natured face was beaming with hope. He was not going to take a refusal. Possibly it was the force of his mind, or some unseen influence many call fate, which made Arthur suddenly decide he would go.

After all, he reasoned, why not? These people are not heathens; it was not demoralizing to associate with them; he would not be here forever, and when he left he need know them no more. Even if they came to his land, which was most unlikely, they would not be foolish enough to think he could entertain them in his home, as they had desired to entertain him here. He had believed before he came, as many another, that they could not even speak his language, that they still continued in the savagery of long past ages, but many of them, he found, had been to the city, had been educated in the government schools, and then returned to their old life because they found in it the joys that they had never found in books. If they were not educated, they spoke the English language freely and could converse with him as Christians, even though they might not know the meaning of the word. Soothing his conscience with the thought that he would do something to reward them for their kindness, on the night of the luau, he was there.

The scene which met his eyes was wierdly fantastic. The immense banyan tree, like a huge octopus or some great hydra-headed monster, round the outspread limbs of which the vines twisted and swung like snakes—was lighted at each end by the yellow flames of torches, held aloft in the hands of smiling native boys. The reflection of the full moon danced on the inwashing tide, leaving the silvery track of her footmarks on the dashing waves. It showed up the carefree faces of the Hawaiians, with the leis about their necks and flowers in their hair. A soft, warm wind swayed the branches of the massive palms, carrying the blue smoke from the oven underground where the pig and meat had been cooking in ti-leaves. The feast was laid upon the sand. Fish fern and guinea grass and flowers formed the tablecloth. Huge bowls of poi, potatoes baked, and savory smelling fish, sea moss, cocoanuts and fruit fresh from the tree was the repast. With appetites tuned up by the sea-air and hours of waiting the natives fell to work, unconscious and uncaring of every thing around them.

Arthur took his seat on the sand, feeling as if he were in another world. Everyone in the little port had turned

out to the great event. He found himself wedged in
between two, happy, laughing women, each feeding
contented looking babies, the miniatures of themselves.
Well, he must join in their festivity. In Rome be tactful
with its customs—and he did not want, as Jack had said,
to make them feel he was a bird from foreign lands. He
tried to dip his finger in the poi and twist it round as
gracefully as they did. Half of it dropped on his lap and
everybody laughed that care-free laugh, for nothing
mattered at a luau. The children might adorn their
fingers with the rings of pineapple or make a trumpet out
of the salt cellar—what was the odds? The joy was in
being free.

Jack Oahu probed his cocoanut, shook the milk into
his glass, and rose to his feet and drank.

"To the glory of the Islands!" he said. "What
beverage could be grander or more refreshing than the
milk our fathers climbed the trees to drink? Or what
more pure and wholesome than the clear, cold waters of
the running stream? Modern inventions there may be.
The men come here from other towns to tell of those who
gained a fortune by inventing sauces to make food swallow with a relish. We do not need that relish; we find
it in the pure air of the Island. The outdoor life asks for
no sauce for hunger. The grandest cooking apparatus
of the day, the most modern oven man invented, would
have no show with ours built in the sun-warmed earth.
No tasty morsel placed upon a plate of gold could equal
food cooked underneath the ground, tied up in ti-leaves,
and served with wet sea moss, gathered from the rocks."
The people smacked their lips with approval and Jack
continued.

"The gods have given us an Island filled with flowers
and fruit and sunshine. They have given us the freedom

of our fathers. What made our fathers free? The freedom of their souls. As children of the sun they knew no
age—they drew their life from that great shining god,
and like well nourished trees, they did not count their
falling leaves—they knew as quickly as they dropped
away, others as beautiful would take their place. They
never asked when they were born, they never thought
when they would die. The sun arose and went to rest,
and then arose again—but always shone. They were
the children of the sun, they owned their sonship. They
lived because they wished for nothing else—only to live
and love. Surfing and sunshine, fruit and flowers, sleeping beneath the starry skies on sun warmed grass, or
golden sands. So did our fathers live—and what of us?
Some of us still live so, but some were drawn to other
lands more beautiful, they thought, than ours. This land
is good enough for me. Some went to seek for gold. They
found it, but it built for them a golden cage. Some died
for fame, some died for wealth. I do not ask the gods
for wealth or fame, I ask for life and love. In other lands
they worry for the things they want. Why should we
worry? We have all we need. In other lands they're sick.
Our fathers knew no sickness. They rose each morning
with the dawn; they washed their faces in the dew. I
want to live just like my fathers lived. I never seek a
grander Heaven than the one that I have found down
here."

Arthur was shocked by this last statement, yet was not
the philosophy of Jesus, "Heaven's kingdom is within
you?"

"So let's be happy," Jack continued as he took his
seat amidst the clapping and the cheers.

The delights of eating were nearly over now. One
after another the people, with satisfied sighs, often bor-

dering on groans, leaned back upon the sand, and some struck up the music of the ukulele. As if in response to this, out from the great branches of the banyan tree, a woman dropped to the ground as lightly as a bird. She wore the grass skirt of the hula, with leis of flowers round her neck and shining in her hair. It was not the dance of the Islands she gave, but a dance of inspiration, wildly beautiful.

Fascinated, Arthur watched her as one might watch a gorgeous bird. Tiptoeing to the water's edge, coquetting with the waves, catching the rays of the moonlight, as she flitted between it and the shadows, she looked more like a spirit of the sea and air than a native of the Island.

Who was she, this wonderful creature that he seemed to know so well? Her dance stopped suddenly. She raised her arms to the light of a golden moon, and her voice range out rich and adoring upon the silent night:

> "Aloha oe, Aloha oe,
> E ke onaona noho ika lipo,
> A fond embrace, a hoi ae au,
> Until we meet again."

No one noticed that Arthur had withdrawn into the shade of the cocoanut tree. He had recognized her as the girl he had seen on the mountain heights, the girl whose blood-red flower still lived among so many more upon his table.

"Again, Lilinoe, again," they shouted as she swung up into the banyan tree and vanished among the branches. She did not return and Arthur was glad of it.

"Too bad," said Iao Hapai. "No girl can dance like Lilinoe—light as the sea foam, and as pretty, but she will never dance for long. She's just a rainbow in the sky; while we are talking of the colors, it has gone. Tune up, let's have a hula."

He stopped and all listened earnestly, for as if in answer to the call of the song, there came the sound of music in the distance, sweet as an angel's touch on harp strings. Music such as Arthur had never heard. It rose and fell, whispering softly, rising again like the call of a soul in pain, then dancing away in a race of notes rapid and sparkling as a rippling laugh.

"It's Ewaliko's music," said Jack. "He must have come down from the mountain."

The boy came strolling towards them, a strange figure weirdly beautiful, with thick black hair overhanging his large and melancholy eyes. He wore nothing but a girdle of leaves fastened around his lithe and graceful body, and a wreath of mountain flowers about his neck.

Arthur found himself wondering how he got such soulful music out of so peculiar an instrument as the one he carried. He wanted to sob with those beautiful notes, he knew not why

The boy was gazing vaguely on the happy scene. He looked like one confused by stepping from a mist into the brilliance of a lighted room.

"I was playing for her," he said, pointing to the path Lilinoe had taken. "Those are her moods. Bright as the stars to look on, though the sky is black around her. Laughing amidst her sobs, smiling amidst her tears, she came into my music. Why? It's always someone's spirit that touches the chords I want to play."

He walked towards the table, still moving like one in a trance. Arthur was reaching forward to see more clearly the outlines of his wonderfully beautiful face. Their eyes met and for a moment they looked at each other. The boy's face changed. All that was beautiful left it. It seemed as if another soul had taken possession

of his body. He backed for a few paces like a tiger ready
to spring.

"Why have you come again to take my prize from
me?" he shouted. "Surely by now I've earned my
treasure. Why did you come to seek her on this Island?"

He was backing slowly as he spoke, the notes of his
music dropping away with his words.

"Shame, shame on you, Ewaliko," called the people.
"How can you spoil our luau?"

He answered nothing, but muttering to himself went
further into the shadow of the banyan tree, still keeping
his eyes on Arthur.

"He has been much better lately," said one of the
women. "He has been quieter and played more."

"Ewaliko is a great soul," spoke up Yee Kui, whose
presence Arthur had not known of till this minute. The
little Chinaman never bothered his master about anything—never asked leave of absence, and had not spoken
of the luau, although he intended to be there. "Ewaliko
lived many lives," he continued, "but he remember too
much. Memory no good, memory make sad. Sun shines
today, no look back when it rained."

He expressed his philosophy with difficulty, but the
happy crowd got it, though it possibly touched Arthur's
soul more than any of theirs. No it was no use to look
back, unless we gained benefit from past experiences.
Lot's wife became stationary forever when she turned to
the city of hopes that were burning, and did not press
forward with the others to scenes that were ahead.

The boy had gone on his way, but the plaintive notes
still lingered on the air.

"There's no music on the Islands like that," said Iao.
"It is the music of the winds and sea. No man can make
his instruments; he forms them himself out of the grasses

and the weeds; he washes them in sea water and dries
them in the sun."

"Has he no parents?" Arthur asked.

Iao shook his head.

"His mother no one knows," he answered. "His father
was an old kahuna who lived up in the mountain caves.
The boy is harmless, but we used to fear his father. He
had the power to pray to death or make well, just as he
chose. He'd won the favor of the gods and knew the
secret passage to their home. There was not anything
he could not do."

"Then why did not he get the gods to help him with
the boy?"

"He said that there was nothing wrong with Ewaliko;
he'd got the double sight, and we had not. It was because
we could not see, we thought him wrong. This was the
only life we knew; but he knew many. His body might
be here, but his soul went wandering to other planes."

One of the older women shuddered. "I was up on
the mountain one day," she said. "I had climbed higher
than I intended to do, the air was so cool, so sweet up
there. I was singing to myself and gathering 'maile,' as
happy as could be, when I turned round and saw the
old man sitting at the entrance to his cave. I was high up,
and it had taken long to climb, but it did not take long
to get down after I'd seen him. I just gave one scream,
and ran for all I was worth. I could not feel my limbs.
How they carried me I never knew. I was like a pebble
rolling, and it seemed as if the heavy clouds had taken
shapes and chased me on all sides. For days and days I
felt their vapory hands upon my hair."

"What did he look like?" asked the people.

"It seemed to me he had three eyes, one right in the
middle of his forehead."

"Lots of people saw that," Jack replied. "He told someone that third eye told him what went on in our homes, so we'd better watch out, or the power would reach us."

"I never felt safe after that until they told me he was dead," the woman went on slowly.

"Hush!" whispered one of the men with superstition. "His spirit may be listening. An eye like that can't die; they say it lives forever. The boy says that he is not dead. He sits in the cave and talks with him, and at night when the heavy storms sweep over the mountain, right on the height that eye shines like a star."

The pleasure-loving people tired of this conversation, picked up their ukuleles and Iao sprang to his feet.

"Come on girls," he said, lightly. "Forget it! Let's have a hula."

Arthur slipped quietly away. He did not want to join in such revelry and he was thankful no one noticed him as he took the pathway under the cocoanut trees to his cottage.

Chapter V

THE PSYCHIC EWALIKO

He was startled suddenly by hearing someone call. From under the shadows of the trees, a figure moved towards him. It was the wild boy of the mountains. His face was calmer now, his mind was on another track.

"Hush," he said softly, raising his hand. "Why does the world make such a noise? These people, how they talk, and laugh, they jabber and then sing, and what about it when they've finished? Which of them are the wiser for it? And you, why don't you listen more; why have you got so much to say?"

Arthur was almost as much taken aback by this second onslaught as he had been by the first, seeing that he had not as yet opened his mouth to the boy, and over at the luau had been the only silent one.

"They call a man a fool if he takes time to listen," he went on, "but the world is full of voices sweeter than our own, voices that tell us many things. Can't you hear them? They want to talk to you, the spirits of the cave."

He had come into the moonlight and his face was transfigured and shining in the silvery rays. He pointed towards a portion of the cliff where the brown rocks looked jagged and in places brilliant red.

"She still bleeds, the great giant," he said. "She died fighting like her ancestors. Look at her open wound, no time can heal it. The flowers may grow out of its crevices —the grass may sprout up and cover it—the vines may twine and twine their arms around it, but the hidden wound will always bleed."

"What wound?" asked Arthur, looking with fascination towards the spot.

"There's where she died," he went on slowly. "See how her lifeblood stained the rocks. The white man came across the sea and took her from us. Our cave, the cave that belonged to us from the beginning. They still cry for her life, the spirits of the old Hawaiians that she sheltered. We played in there when we were little children—played one life in and out again, and then came back to play. She was our rock of ages in the storm, and when we came down from the mountain, our protection from the cold. She was our guardian angel of the night, she spread her wings about us while we slept, but they took her from us, and she will come back no more."

He stopped and shivered slightly. Arthur was recalling the history Jack had told him.

"They took the cave away to give you something better," he said kindly. "The natives told me that they had to have a wharf to land the boats. The cave was useless, and it took up too much room. They could not build with such obstruction. Man has to blast the rocks, and often fell the trees to make way for the things more needful."

The boy looked at him sadly for a moment. "Has man to kill his brother to make room for other lives?" he asked. "Stand by and see your brother shot, let the world tell you that they'll give you something better. They came to blow her up, those people living far across the waves. They brought the shell and powder. We saw the landing of their boats and we went down to bid a fond farewell."

He paused again. Arthur could see the tears were wet upon his cheeks, the tears of a native who loves every spot of his land.

"We wanted to die with her, some of us. We sat under her shelter till the executioners had come. We kissed the vines that twisted their arms in love around her rocks; we said good-bye to the long, waving ferns that we had often gathered from her walls; we sat on the old stone throne for the last time, and then——"

"And then?" asked Arthur, forgetting his fear of the boy in the interest of the story.

"And then the god of the deep sent down a mighty storm. The sea grew wild, the waves sprang up in anger, rushing towards the shore like armies shouting for revenge. Clouds big as mountains rolled across the sky, lashed by the black wings of a screaming wind. Then like a deluge down came the rain, blowing from North to South, from East to West, striking the people on all sides, whichever way they ran for refuge. Peal after peal of thunder rent the air—bolt after bolt of fire hissed into the sea. The lightning with sword of vengeance smote the trees in twain and ripped the leaves of the banana into ribbons. "We saw boats tossed like leaves upon the highest crests of waves, and then tossed down to disappear, never to rise again. The earth began to tremble with the force. Black darkness threw her mantle over all, rolling the ocean, sky and mountains into one—and then it seemed the end had come. "But out of the shock of the thunder and through the shouting of the mighty waves, I heard what others did not—I heard a voice sweet as a mountain bird's—so soft, so low, yet audible to me above the storm. It was the voice of 'Wahine,' the spirit of the cave. Long had she lived within its walls and held the open house for us. You do not know her story, yet she sheltered you when moons were young. Why does the world forget, and have to learn its lesson all again?

Arthur stood waiting for the story—amazed that he should care to hear.

"More than two thousand sunrises ago," The boy continued, "Wahine came across the water. She was a queen of many lands, proud, arrogant and beautiful, wanting the best things for herself, and wiping out by cruelty and death all who were called more beautiful than she.

"The gods grew angry at her wicked life and, as her punishment, made her invisible to mortal eye. Then everyone was seeking for the vanished queen, though nobody regretted her, and no one wept for her, because she had been cruel to them all. By her own table she stood invisible, and saw another crowned where she had sat. She heard the shouts and cheers of her subjects. 'This queen, they said, 'is the one we wanted. She is so sweet, so beautiful and kind. We could not love the wicked queen, Wahine.' And they put a cloak of scarlet feathers round her and draped her with the fairest flowers. At her own table the queen Wahine sat, invisible, and no one came to wait on her nor serve her. She tried to box the servant's ears for disregarding her commands, but they only thought it was a heavy wind, and ran to close the windows.

"Weary of hearing others praised and having to stand by unnoticed, she stepped into her canoe and paddled out to sea, thinking the water might be kinder to her than her so-called friends. She had never sailed alone before, and the rising tide began to frighten her. Boat after boat, went past, coming so close they touched her paddle, which was invisible to them. In vain she called for help. No one could hear her voice. Day after day she drifted on the lonely waves, longing and praying for a sight of land. Then in the distance, suddenly, she saw the green of waving palms, the cocoanuts and golden sands. She dropped her paddle, threw her arms aloft and called into the air: "God of the waves and seas and winds, let me touch land again, and all my life I will give in sacrifice for others. No more for self I live. I live to serve."

"Her cry, unheard by mortal ear, was carried quickly to the gods. A wave spread out and lifted her with her canoe as if on wings, carrying her onwards, onwards towards the massive mountains towering aloft like giants in the distance. She covered her face, as with a mighty sweep the wave descended throwing her landward in a cloud of foam. She rose unhurt and rubbed the water from her eyes and looked around. Blue Heavens smiled across the sand where we are standing, and palms and flowers waved 'Aloha.'

"The fishermen came by. They were talking of the unexpected tidal wave. 'It did no damage,' all agreed, but just look at the mountain. See how it cleft the rocks apart. Look at the lovely cave of refuge Neptune has prepared.'

"The Queen was standing at the entrance, just where her canoe had struck. They did not see her, but they thanked the good gods for the wave which by its mighty force had broken apart the rocks and scooped out this great place of shelter for them.

"So moons rolled in the sky, and stars went out and shone again, and still 'Wahine' gave her life in service for us, but she was only visible to few. She sat upon her throne and welcomed us to her shelter by the warmth of her heart. She decorated the walls with ferns and moss and gathered the sea shells and hid them in the crevices for little children. It was her voice that I heard in pleading for the Island—offering her life for us when Neptune would have swept us by his mighty wrath into the depths. She rose like thin blue smoke out of the entrance, stretching her hands of light towards the sea. Then all grew still. Her soft form melted into Heaven's blue—the wind grew gentle as her voice—the rain ceased suddenly, and with one foot on sea and one on land a rainbow stepped across the sky. The gods had claimed their sacrifice; our land was saved. Neptune fought for the cave no more. It died, but it died fighting. It was a long and slow surrender. It was so strong, so old, it held out to the last."

Arthur was recalling the practical history Jack had told him.

"They had filled the cave with gunpowder, so I heard," he said, "but the storm and heavy rain had made it damp so that it was slow to ignite." The boy talked on as if he had not heard.

"We would awaken in the night and hear the groans and shudders—the long, low rumble of the stones falling on all sides. She went down like a giant stabbed on every hand, losing ground each moment, yet though a sacrifice for us, longing to live. Hush," he continued, raising his hand again. "The spirits of the old Hawaiians still wail for her. Don't you hear? They are calling, calling for the past."

Arthur did not know whether it was the sudden wind in the branches of the palm trees, or the waves rushing through the hidden crevices of rocks, but the long, weird moan came again and again.

He looked towards the spot where the cave had been. He saw the mighty gashes where her body had been torn from the overhanging heights. The stones and earth surrounding were red as lifeblood flowing from an open wound.

Once more the boy looked towards him. The wild light came into his eyes. "And you," he said, "why did you come back here? Why should you take the things I love? You came before, you came into our land and plucked the prettiest flower, you carried her away, you left me in the darkness."

"I?" answered Arthur. "What do you mean? I never saw your land before. Why should I want your women?"

The boy's laugh broke his sentence—"Yes, why?" he answered, "but you do. You say you never knew our land?—look over there, and you'll remember."

As if some strange magnetic force had drawn him, he turned in the direction where the boy was pointing. He saw the shadow of himself upon the rocks reflecting in the mirror of the ocean. He knew it was himself, although the form was strong and handsome, and the limbs were beautiful and full of power. He saw the girl of the grass skirt, radiant and lovely stepping from the sea. He saw the boy who stood beside him, princely and wonderful and strong. He saw a ship sail inwards with white sails glittering in the light, and then he saw himself stand with the girl upon the deck. He saw her arms reach out in love to what was left behind.

"You took her," said the boy, "and what did I send after you? All you are full of now—sickness and misery and want. You said that you did not remember, but you cannot say so any more."

The scene had faded as quickly as it came. Arthur breathed deeply, rubbed his eyes like one awakening from a dream.

'Maybe it won't be this time," he went on, sadly, "but one will come for her more beautiful than I have eyes to see, and when she goes with him my life goes like a stricken flower."

He walked away, and Arthur stood alone. For a moment he was unable to think of anything except the weirdness of the place in which he found himself. He looked from right to left. Above him was a sky of shining light. Beneath his feet the silvery sands, shadowed by the long forms of giant palms, and away in the distance the red glow of the torches, the sound of ukuleles, and the wild dance of the natives in their hula. He was glad to get into his cottage and shut himself up in his room.

CHAPTER VI

MEMORIES OF THE MOUNTAIN HOME

Next morning Arthur did not feel inclined to go down to the beach. He sat on the sheltered lanai looking across the fields of glistening sugar-cane, at the calm blue waters of the sea. Two dragon flies chased each other in the sun light and flitted merrily beneath the leaves of the banana tree. A long-horned, black and white, straight-backed cow munched contentedly in front of him. The mud-wasps were carrying their masonry to the top of the window. Hens gossiped noisily over their lunch, but Arthur's canvas was full of colors that were new—he was not even thinking of his health. Above all other features in the gorgeous luau of the night before, one picture stood out clearly, and that was the wild dance of the girl.

A sense of pain was in his soul—a horror born of a small conventional life which could not adjust itself to the free life of the Islands. He thought of the kindness in her voice when she had helped him to find his way along the beach, the first night that he met her. He could not associate this character with the shameless woman in the hula skirt.

He had never seen her after that first meeting, but every morning just at day-break, some one had left a lei of flowers by his door. Flowers freshly gathered—flowers of the dawn, with the dew wet upon them. To a romantic soul there would have been something wonderfully poetic in those fairy wreaths and horse-shoes placed each day

55

by unseen hands. But poetry outside the written verse was far removed from Arthur. He wondered whether he should acknowledge them as a gift or else refuse politely to accept them.

"It is their sweet custom," the Chinaman had said, when he saw the hesitation on his master's face. "It is 'Aloha,' to a stranger on the Islands, and shows that you have won their hearts with love."

He remembered that there had been no "lei" at his door this morning, and he felt glad it was so. Somehow he knew instinctively that the girl he met upon the beach had placed those flowers there. She was a hula dancer— a wild girl of the Islands—this might be done for money —he decided he must settle up her bill.

But Lilinoe had not forgotten her gift. She came by the side path across the fields. She was later in bringing it this morning. She had been down to the beach to pick the sea-plants from the shallow water, and mixing them with tiny colored shells, had formed one of her prettiest leis. She came so gently that he did not hear her, and before he knew, the lei was around his neck. She clapped her hands at his surprise and laughed just like a child, as he quietly removed it.

"What did you take it off for?" she asked, lightly. "Don't you like shells and weeds? I thought that they would be a change from flowers."

"They are a little damp," he answered, fumbling lamely for an excuse before he gave the reason in his soul.

She laughed again, the care-free laugh of the Hawaiian. "The damp couldn't hurt you—the shells are full of health and love."

His eyes unconsciously were resting on them. The same power seemed to reach him that came each morning with the flowers. It softened the hard feeling in his heart, softened the scorn and the contempt of lives as free as hers.

"You have been very kind to think of me," he said. "I do not know your customs here. I have appreciated the flowers, and if you let me know your charge——"

His purse was in his hand.

Her big black eyes were asking for an explanation.

"I mean, what money do I owe you for these flowers?"

She looked at the cold dollars—then out across the sun-bathed Island, where in the richest colors, thousands of flowers blazed God's love. He thought he saw a shade of sadness cross her face.

"Money?" she hesitated. "Money for flowers? But they would not want to give their lives for money." She reached her hand out as she spoke and plucked a fragrant allamanda, flaming bright gold beneath the brilliant light. She kissed its open petals as one might kiss the lips of a little child whose tender feelings had been hurt. "They live, because they love us," she said gently—"but if they had to sell their lives, they would not want to live again."

He smiled at her philosophy. "You talk as if they had a soul like we have," he said, grimly.

"A soul?" she hesitated at the words. "You mean that lovely something made of light that goes out when we leave our body. Yes—flowers have a soul—I've seen it —it rises on their perfume and floats away into the garden of the Gods."

A moment's silence followed her speech, then Arthur said more kindly:

"You people are a superstitious race—great believers in romance."

"Don't you believe it, too?" she asked. "Don't you believe that all things live again?"

"Well, yes—in one way, I believe that if the flower sheds its petals, the life will still live in the root. The rays of light fall from the sun, but the great ball holds its throne up in the heavens. But speaking of a soul, we touch on different ground. God gave the soul to human beings alone."

"Did He? I wonder why?"

"We do not need to question, these things are an accepted fact."

"I wonder why," she said again. "I wonder why He thought that human beings were worthier than the flowers."

"God created us in His own image," he went on, glad that he seemed to be gaining ground. "We were His last creation and his greatest."

"Why did your God make us the last, and why when He had made so many lovely things, did He give the soul to us alone? The flowers must be as much a part of Him. I used to think they grew because the sun-god kissed the earth."

Her persistency was wearying, still she continued: "We're always fighting for ourselves and wanting something better. The flowers never ask for anything—they only live to give. I don't know any life as selfless as a flower's. The little blossoms shining in the grass like stars —the jessamine that climbs the roof—the kowalis in their gowns of white and pink—the scented haw—the flame of Jack-o'-lantern, all asking to be twisted into leis of love. I've stopped by hedges of night-blooming cereus, and they've smiled on me like angels' faces smiling through the dark. Oh, flowers have a soul, I've seen it. Some come to heal, some come to live, but all come here to serve."

"You have much to learn," he answered, quietly.

"And much that I don't want to learn," she said. "It would not make me very happy to think that souls belonged to us alone."

His eyes rested for a moment upon the flower that she had pinned upon his coat when they first met. Yee Kui had changed the water, and put it beside the window sill. The light was shining on its brilliant petals, still fresh and beautiful though all the other flowers were dead.

"That is a mountain flower," she said. "It gives its life to heal the sick. It grows upon the heights in crevices unknown, it only blooms at night time, and is very difficult to find."

Arthur was looking at it with amazement. It came to him with sudden surprise that days had passed since she had given him that flower, and yet the scent was just as sweet, the petals just as fresh.

"Strange it should live so long," he said. "I never saw one like it."

She reached through the open window and touched the crimson leaves. "You say that flowers have not a soul," she answered, "and yet that flower asked to come to you. You may not crush the lifeblood from its petals, but you take the sweetness from its heart.

"I did not want to give it to you at first," she went on slowly. "It is so hard to find them, and there are so few."

"But are not others quite as beautiful?" he said. "That is a hardy flower, of course. It probably outlives the family, but surely other flowers would be as good."

This time she did not seem to hear him. Her eyes were fixed upon the flower. He was glad to turn the conversation. He wanted to speak about the doings of the night before, and she gave him the opportunity when she asked "Did you enjoy our luau and what did Ewaliko say to you?"

"Luau—? yes, it was all right," he said, not wanting to evince too great an interest in their doings, "but that boy Ewaliko puzzles me—it strikes me he has lost his mind."

"Or found it," she replied. "Perhaps he thinks too much; he thinks about many lives. I don't do that, this life is very beautiful to me; I live it now, I have learned to forget."

He did not follow her, he just continued—"The boy seems educated, he can speak quite well; was he in school?"

She laughed at the idea. "Not in the place that you call school. He could not learn from books, he learns from other things—from other people."

"And yet they say he does not associate with others much?"

She smiled at his want of understanding, and changed the subject quickly as she asked "How did you like my dance? You went away when I had finished, and I was waiting for you in the old place where I met you at the time of which Ewaliko spoke."

Her talk was vague and senseless to him. He answered sharply and practically enough—"I did not like your dance at all. Where did you ever learn such foolish things?"

"To dance? We all dance as we walk or swim. You danced once yourself."

"Not that I know of."

"Something you have forgotten," she replied. "You have lived in many different lands for many lives, but we don't know your dances here. You think us strange, but we are not strange, we are just ourselves."

Yes, that was true. He must remember that he was in another land—must try to help and not condemn these people.

"You have forgotten," she said slowly, I had forgotten too—but I had a flash of memory for a moment last night in the dance, beneath the banyan tree, but Ewaliko does not forget, and memory makes him sad." She waved her hand in front of her eyes for a moment, and surprised him by waving it in front of his.

"It's gone now," she said suddenly. "Let's talk of to-day."

"Tell me about your parents," he said, surprised at the weird interest he was feeling in this girl. "You have had an education, yet you told me once you never went to school."

"My mother was a lady," she replied. "She taught us everything we knew. She had seen your land across the water, but this land was her home. My grandmother, they said, was of royal birth, but they never told us much about it, and it did not matter anything to me. Whether my mother wore a pretty gown or hula skirt, she always looked a queen. I guess she was real cute and pretty as a child, for when the white people came here they saw her playing on the beach and wanted to adopt her. My grandfather was willing she should go, for he had lots of children in the hut, and maybe lots to come. So they took her over the big water into a lovely home. Sometimes she used to tell us all about it. It must have been a funny place to live—they wore so many clothes, and at their meals they put a tablecloth upon their knees as well as on the table. She had a maid to wait on her and pretty things to wear, but she was never happy. She wanted the grass hut and sunshine. Snow fell where they were living, and in the winter it was cold—the flowers were dead, the birds were all asleep.

"She learnt to read and write, to play and sing. She learnt so many things that she forgot, and lots that she remembered. But she was homesick for the Islands. She had played with my father on the beach and she could not forget him. He used to come to her in dreams, and when the wind blew cold at night, she seemed to hear his call come through it. One night it wakened her—that call. She saw the Island and the blue canoe in which they sailed and hid beneath, when they were children. She saw him standing by it, waving to her. He was older now, for he was grown, but she knew it was her little comrade. She could wait no longer, and she came to him."

"And was she happy when she got back here?"

"Happy? Of course, This was her land—the land where she was born, and all her people lived. She found her playmate of the past, and he became my father."

Arthur was following her story.

"Yes, she was best in her own land," he said. "A wild flower will not flourish in a hot-house."

"They went to live up on the mountain. They built their hut where we were born. It was so beautiful. We seemed to have the world all to ourselves. Few people ever knew we lived there. Rocks hid our home, and palms and bushes. We had no trail cut to our door—only the goats could find the way.

"You never saw the sunrise here, like we saw it on the mountain. We used to climb far up above to look at the bright colors. The sky was just a blaze of fire, and under us were the clouds. It seemed like we were sailing in a great big ship, in the middle of a golden sea. Sailing with thousands of menahunes and fairies, with robes made out of shining beads. Somehow we could not talk when we looked at the sunrise—it was too great and grand for words. We hardly ever went down to the little town, and when we did, we wanted to get back. All that we loved we found up there—sunsets and birds and trees and flowers, moonlight in which the brownies danced. Cool winds which carried the scents of pines and sweet smelling maile, big white stars to look down on us, and the great, strong mountain to protect us."

"But how did you get fed?"

She laughed at such a question. "How do the animals and birds get fed? There was fruit enough in the forests and on the mountain slopes. We drank the milk of the cocoanut and the fresh waters of the springs. We used to take our morning shower in the waterfalls. We did not wear much clothing, for we did not need it. Our mother taught us reading from the books she brought across the water, she taught us how to write and spell. We learned because she wanted us to learn, but it seemed to me we had no need, for I thought that we would spend our lives forever on that lovely mountain."

"And no one lived up there except yourselves?"

"Only the Kahunas, and they kept people away. There were hidden precipices among the trees and bushes, and many thought that they were cut as traps by these men who lived in caves behind the denseness of the foliage. They lived in the wild, rugged jungle, no one could tell exactly where."

"The Kahunas," he interrupted. "They talked of one last night. Tell me about them."

"The Kahunas were dreaded by the people of the Island. They had the power to pray to death a person whom they did not like. When a man was troubling him, the King sent word to the Kahuna. If possible he got a piece of that man's hair, or maybe his finger nail. The Kahuna had to know his name, and then he called it, and gathered all the power of every god, and sent it forth like a tornado, and it went whirling through space and struck the man, and he fell dead. Some men they prayed to death by bits, and then they lingered, and they suffered. The people were afraid of them, but we were not. I loved them and they were always kind to me.

"My mother said that I was not a happy baby, and she could not tell the reason why. She cradled me and nursed me, but when I wakened after sleep, I used to sob and sob—not like an ordinary baby, but in a way which made her take me in her arms and sob with me, she knew not why. "One morning when she awoke she found me missing. I was learning then to creep and crawl. She rushed out on the mountain—calling—looking everywhere for me. She had never gone near the homes of the Kahunas, but there was one who stood upon the hillside in the morning, beating his drum and chanting to the sunrise. He was so old—about two hundred, so the natives said—but he lived and prayed out on the mountains—just lived with life—and *lived*. My mother found me sitting at his feet. He had his face turned to the sunrise and she always said its rays had wrapped me round, and I was encircled in a golden light. He did not seem to notice me: he never stopped his chanting for a moment. But every morning at the sunrise I was missing, and they always found me at the old man's feet, encircled in the same gold ring of light.

"One morning when my mother came for me, he stopped his chanting and they talked. He told her I would cry like that no more, for love had set me free. I was, he said, a lonely soul, carrying the memories of past lives, and when I slept I went into those lives and came back feeling strange and sad—sad as she felt across the water. He seemed to know her story without telling. He said another prayer and told her that she need not fear my future, because I bore love's conquering sign, and I would triumph over all.

"She never worried after that. I could go where I liked, and she knew that I was safe.

"I grew to love the old Kahuna. I used to sit with him inside his cave. It was far away, far out behind the bushes. We had to drop down many a gulch to find it. Inside it all looked dark at first, but when I sat with him awhile, I saw the light. A kind of phosphorant moss grew on the ceiling. It shone like tiny moons in a black sky, and the gleams from it fell downward in long rays, shining and bright as spiders' webs in the sunshine of the morning.

"I never tired of sitting there with him. I never tired of wandering with him all over the mountain. He taught me how to greet the dawn, and how to meet the sunrise with a prayer. He showed me how to call the power, and how to understand my dreams.

"On moonlight nights we went to pick the healing herbs and flowers. None knew where these grew, except the old Kahuna. It did not matter if the moon went in, he could always find them. He used to stand still for a moment and listen till he heard their call. If you had been there, too, you would have known that flowers have souls. Souls that smile through their smiling eyes and parted lips—souls that can talk to you without a voice.

"Other Kahunas prayed to death, but he prayed people well. He would not pray for single individuals— he prayed for the world."

"Where is he now?" asked Arthur, trying to conceal the interest he felt in her story.

"He lives," she whispered, softly, "but no one can approach his door. The people have forgotten him, or so it seems. He lives away up on the heights, hidden by all the trees and gulches. He lives alone. He lives to pray."

"And do you ever go to see him?"

"I have not been for many moons. He can reach people better at a distance—he does not want the human face and hands; he wants that shining light, you call the soul."

"Does he speak any language but his own?"

"He can speak many, but when he has spoken, he forgets. All things, he says, are ready for us when we need them. Don't overload the vessels. The things we want are born with our desire."

Arthur was looking steadily at her. She was a riddle that he could not read.

"Why did you come down from the mountain if you were so happy with those peculiar people who had made their homes up there?" he asked.

She laughed at the *"peculiar people."*

"They weren't peculiar people," she replied. "Why did I come down from the mountain?" A shade of sorrow such as he had never seen upon her face, clouded it for a moment. Her eyes turned to the flower shining upon the window sill.

"I would have stayed up there forever," she said, softly, "but many changes came. The angels of the night called for my mother. She was still young, and, oh, so beautiful, but she told us that the count of years was over, and there was something wonderful awaiting her. She did not know just what it was, but she said it lay behind the sunset.

"We were sitting on the mountain side one Summer evening. The air had never seemed so fresh, the flowers had never smelt so sweet. The stars were white as blossoms in the sky. The sea looked like a sea of gold— so calm, so full of rest—we might have walked its shining floor. We generally sang at night time and played our ukulele, but tonight we were not singing—we wanted to sit still and listen. We seemed to be expecting something. I had never seen my mother look so beautiful. We had put a wreath of snowy jessamine upon her hair. It flashed like a crown of jewels in the moon's clear light. Suddenly my father raised his hand. He said he heard a voice far in the distance. My mother smiled and answered that she heard it, too.

" 'It is my guardian angels,' she said softly, 'and they call for me.'

No forms were visible—only a cloud, soft, white and beautiful dropped low upon the mountain. I watched it drawing nearer, its light growing brighter every moment, till like a brilliant sun it flashed before my eyes, and then I saw it was no cloud, but a form in dazzling white, with outstretched shining wings, which closed around our dear one until she, too, became a blaze of light, and after that I knew no more."

She stopped. Her face had caught the radiance of the past experience and it made her beautiful beyond expression.

"Could this be," Arthur thought, "the dancer of the night before?"

"We laid her to rest by the little hut where she had lived upon the heights, between the sunset and the sea. We covered her with the mountain flowers—sweet-scented violets, silver sword and moss and lichens. It was a night just like it had been when the guardian angels

came, so still, so calm, so pretty. She had promised she
would send a sign to show us she was with us, and while
we stood out on the mountain, rain, soft as dew fell from
the sky, and right above the silver moon a rainbow broke,
and then another, and another. They disappeared and
came again, like angels smiling through the colors of
the sky. Then in the tree above our heads a bird broke
out in song. I never knew what kind of bird. I never
heard a song so sweet. It seemed to me that her dear
spirit was singing to us through those rich and lovely
notes. She had promised us a sign to tell us that she
lived again—and we had got it—she was happy."

Again she paused. Then Arthur asked:

"Your father—what of him?"

"He wasn't long to follow. He always said he heard
her call, and one night he went out to meet her. They
both sleep on the mountain side—while we——."

"How many are there of you?" Arthur asked.

"Only my brother and myself."

"Your brother? Is he with you now?"

"Not now," she answered, and then she said no more,
but once again her eyes turned to the flower.

Chapter VII

THE KAHUNA

The revival of old history had made Lilinoe long for scenes of the past. She kept no record of years. Time was counted by events, and much had happened since she visited the old Kahuna. Often she had sensed his presence with her; Many times had heard his voice in the chanting to the sunrise; Even in her secret sorrow which she had hidden from her kindest friends, she had not sought his aid, though she felt instinctively that he must know. Once he had said to her in the few talks they had together: "We cannot move until the stars are ready." She had gone up the mountain many times and drawn very near his door, but unseen hands seemed to prevent her entrance. It was easy to set forth this morning, so she knew the time had come.

Down on the beach she met Ewaliko. He was gathering shells like a happy, natural child—the events of the luau all forgotten. His moods changed like the weather, but Lilinoe understood him. She knew as the old Chinaman had said, that he was wandering through **too many** lives in one. She knew he was happier on the mountains, talking to the birds and flowers and sleeping in the starlight. People distressed and excited him, and it was always her effort to get him back to his own environment. He came towards her smiling and bound a lei of seaweed round her neck, then pointed across the water.

"The waves are happy in the sunshine," he said gently, "See how they love the sky."

"And how the sky loves them," she answered, always falling in with his sweet fancies, as she looked upon the bright reflection of Heaven's glorious blue.

"Come, Ewaliko," she continued, as she put her arm around him—"we are going up the mountain—you and I."

He did not attempt to refuse. In her presence he was always sweet and gentle as a little child. Looking into her face with eyes that smiled like a flower he might have been another character from the wild boy of the luau. They climbed like mountain goats from peak to peak, pelting each other now and again with flowers, or twisting a lei of maile about their necks. On one high peak they paused and looked down on the calm blue waters far below. The boy laid his head on her shoulder as he whispered:

"You are my sky, and I the sea. O, would there could be no more storms, but all just like today—sweet peace and rest."

She knew his mind was drifting to a past which she did not remember. She took his hand in hers, and they went on again, until the scene began to fade and a soft white fog dropped round about them. The walking grew more difficult, and then again they paused and Ewaliko turned towards her He never went beyond this point. He had an unvoiced fear of the great heights. They met in one long fond embrace, and then he sadly asked:

"How many more times shall we walk this way? How long before he claims you—takes you away— and leaves me desolate?"

"No one will take me, Ewaliko," she replied. "Why do you contemplate such a thing? How could I ever leave the land I love?"

A light of joy came to his eyes, but faded just as quickly as it came.

"But he is coming for you," he responded. "I often think that he is here. I sit out in the darkness and try to get the vision of his face, but somehow I see nothing, only the smile of the stars."

She put her fingers on his forehead and rubbed them lovingly across his brow.

"Forget it, Ewaliko," she said, gently. "You're wandering to a history long ago. The white man from the coast maybe upset you. Forget him now—think of your music and the flowers."

Today her influence did not reach him.

"He took you once—that white man," he responded. "He may not take you just like that again, but he builds the bridge for you to cross. I knew twelve moons ago that he was coming. I saw it in my waking dreams."

He turned away with a sigh, which melted into notes of music, plaintive as a wind among the pines.

"Dear Ewaliko," she said, sadly, as she looked at his receding figure, slim as a reed, graceful and beautiful in form. "Why should he get these nervous fancies? I go away from here? Away from this dear mountain—away from the grass hut—away from *him*—my brother? Never."

She shook off the thought and climbed still higher—feeling her footsteps over tracks unbroken and stones hidden by moss and scrubby bushes, until the land below was blotted out and through the wastes of clouds she found her way to the heights.

The hut she sought was built inside a cave—the great, strong walls of which sheltered it from the mountain storms and heavy rains. Outside, the old Kahuna sat. With sunshine up above—and down below, the banks of clouds, he looked like some great sea god, seated on a throne of silver crested foam. His brow was marked by many lines—not ugly lines—but lines of strength written in powerful story by the pen of life. White as the silver sword growing on the highest altitude, his unkempt hair fell over his shoulders and his bright eyes shone like clear stars, unclouded by a mist.

No one for years had come to him, but he did not seem surprised to see Lilinoe. His smile to her was very kind, though for a little while they did not speak. There was something divinely beautiful in the unbroken silence. The rest to her was sweet as it had been when as a little crying child she crept into his understanding heart. Yet in one way how lonely it must be for him away up here, with no companionship beyond the insects, birds and trees. Her mind went quickly to another, still more lonely, and the sudden tears filled her eyes.

He got her thought and his voice was kind and sympathetic as he answered:

"Human companionship is very sweet, but the soul must know there is no distance. The hand of flesh is but the petal for the flower's scent. We long for lips that cling to ours, for arms that hold us in a fond embrace. But love need not take visible expression. The things most powerful are the things invisible to mortal eyes. You came to me to ask for favors from the gods. The gods do not have favorites. I spend my time in prayer—but not for individuals. I do not pray alone for this small Island, for it is but one tiny flake of snow among myriads on the mountain heights. Worlds within worlds and worlds beyond us; Worlds that out outward eyes have never seen; Worlds that out inner sight is not prepared for; Worlds filled with voices sweet, and glories unrevealed. To send our love out on the wings of prayer to

one alone would not be right, for love created and
embraces all. The sun shines on the weeds and flowers
alike. To that great force which some name love, all
things must be the same."

"And yet do not the gods love some more dearly than
others, and grant them many favors?" asked Lilinoe.

"No, some love the gods more dearly and walk within
the knowledge of the laws of the creation, and thus they
draw those so-called favors to them. The man who does
not know our land will miss its hidden fruits, but the
native walks in the paths where he will find them."

But when I was a little child you prayed for me,"
she said.

"Not for you as an individual," he replied. "Not for
you as a sweet and pretty little child who pleased my
fancy. You healed yourself as all of us must do. Love
was all round about you, but you cried for the love of
former lives—a love which your newly incarnated soul
thought lost. But nothing in the universe is lost. The
stars may vanish on a misty night, but when the mist has
driften they are there. The love you craved had never
left you, but you were groping for connection. My prayer
went out for every soul in the vast universe. Those who
were ready felt its power. One of those souls you were.
You had the open door. Love entered in. It was no
favoritism."

"My brother——" she began.

"You need not tell me. He will meet salvation when
the time has come. Why do we need to hurry things
when we go on forever? To me there is no time, no
count of seasons. Your brother is just one flower in the
great and beautiful lei of life, and because he appeals
more to the human senses that is no reason why I should
pause by him. In some way he has missed the path, for

love has never placed him where he is. The wave of prayer goes out, traveling through space with the rapidity of light. It pauses over none, but if the boy is ready, he will receive the power and use it. He will flourish on it like you did. It will build his house afresh, for love wills no one to be sick. Love would not wish to see its loved one suffer. If he believes in love alone, he will be well."

He paused and they sat in the silence broken only by the gentle talking of the birds and the whispered answers of the leaves and flowers. Time slipped away on angel's wings while in his presence.

"Tell me," he said at last, "what colors are in the sunset."

She did not know the sun was setting, but already the sky above and the cloud banks beneath were brilliant as a crater fire. She placed her hands over her eyes as she looked into the light. Colors of all descriptions flashed with a rapidity which made words weak. Blazes of gold, bright as a plover's wing, deepening to orange, and fading into primrose tints—touched here and there by fragments of brilliant clouds, like the fallen blossoms of the flame poinsettia, Lines of crimson, and pink delicate as sea shells—Again rich purple shades, royal as the robes of kings, toning to hues as soft and velvety as the petals of a gold-eyed pansy.

Without a word she looked upon the swiftly changing scene, wishing that nature's artist would not work so fast. It seemed as if in one brief moment all had come and gone, or were caught up in a flame of dazzling white—so bright, so beautiful that like the stars in the full rays of noonday, each color lost itself within the blaze.

"What colors do you see?" he asked again.

She put her hands above her eyes and tried to look into the shining brightness.

"I don't see any " she replied. "They have all gone.
I can see nothing but a great white light."

"My prayer is answered, then," he said. "The time
is nearer than I thought."

He lifted up his hands in blessing and rising to his
feet, stepped forth into the flame, until it shone around
him in a brilliant aura, through which the colors flashed
like rainbows in the sun. His eyes were bright with
prophecy, as far away he pointed to the unseen promised
land.

"Look at the colors now, my child," he said, "They
are broken by the prism. These colors represent the
different nations—divided, separated, often at war—yet
all belonging to the one immortal flame. "Like sheep
they have wandered from the shepherd, driven astray
like clouds by every wind. Unconscious of their value they
have broken the best gifts of the gods—have left their
own bright fields of promise to fight for another's gain.
But all good gifts are equally divided, and when man
thinks he gains another's ground, he loses that much of
his own. But they are coming back to the beginning—
they are coming to build where they destroyed. They are
coming like tired fighters from the field. They will erect
where they tore down. No longer shall man fall for
woman's love, but lifted on the white wings of its purity,
shall be inspired to noble acts and deeds. And by this
power shall woman lead the nations.

"Upon our Island a woman native shall arise. Her
light shall be bright as the chariot of the sun. Brighter
than Pele's fires it shall shine. The men shall follow her,
but she shall know no man, but shall give to all, the vision
of an isle more glorious than Wakea—where the sword
shall be no more, and men shall walk as gods. From shore

to shore the light of her vision shall travel, until like a golden girdle, it has encircled the whole earth."

He ended his prophecy suddenly, and returning to his hut, he shut the door.

Lilinoe stood alone, enveloped in the clouds. The sunset had vanished. There was a bitter coldness in the air, but her heart was full of a strange rapture—something too wonderful to understand.

CHAPTER VIII

THE HAWAIIAN HEALER

The days that followed were somewhat trying to
Arthur. In the case of a severe illness one might have
called it the getting better stage. He was impatient with
his life and his surroundings. He was tired of the house,
tired of the beach. The very beauty of the Island
nauseated him, like the heavy perfume of an over-scented
valentine. The vitality of the natives made him fretful.
He was even out of temper with his faithful little Chinaman, and spoke sharply to him more than once, con-
cerning his slow ways. Yee Kui took it all without a
word. Sucked his pipe a little harder, and continued to
watch his master with the sympathy that one might
watch a plant growing on foreign soil.

He had not seen Lilinoe since the morning after the
luau, and he assured himself that he was glad.

The fishermen had been very kind, but even with
them he felt he must not form too close acquaintance—
it might annoy him in the future.

The future! But after all, what did the future hold
for him? How little he had thought of it. Others had
made him believe that on this plane he had no future—
that his miserable existence as an invalid would end in
death. A future! It gave him energy to think of it! But
even so, if life's path stretched before him, what was
there he could do? Who needed him in this great world,
where there were others so much better? This thought

stepped in, and wiped out his bright hope with cruel fingers. If he should leave the Island, where would he go, and what would be his aim? If he dropped out of existence, who would there be to care? He smiled satirically. Friends of the family would say with resignation: "Well, poor soul, he's better off. He was always suffering, anyway."

A sense of deep resentment crept over him at the narrowness of his life—its little interest, its limited love.

At this moment nature seemed in sympathy with his mood. The sky was suddenly overcast, a heavy shower began to fall; he got up hurriedly and walked towards the cottage. In the distance he could hear the sound of a ukulele. A native boy and girl came down the walk and stopped to kiss beneath the majenta flowers of the bougainvilla arch. Arthur turned away with a sense of disgust which might have been translated "pain." It was natural, he supposed, but he had never known such things. No one had kissed him, even as a child. In his caged and lonely boyhood he had often craved a love fondly expressed. Respect he had always felt for the aunt who had spent her time in Sunday School work, visiting and sewing for bazaars, and who would pat him on the head when she went out, tell him to do his lessons well and not get cold. But love, what had it ever meant to him, he who had never known a friend?

Somehow he did not want to go indoors; the clouds had cleared; the shower had spent itself as quickly as the tears of a child. Sunshine and rainbow clasped hands in the sky. He took the path by the rocks and stood there thinking. The fishermen in the distance waved their hands to him, but he scarcely noticed. His mind was so occupied that he did not even watch his footing, and in a moment he had slipped and fallen. Jack Oahu was the first to reach him. Arthur had quickly gained his feet but his face looked white, and his hand was resting on his arm.

"It was a bad fall," said the fisherman, "and you look shaken." His touch was tender and his voice as sympathetic as a woman's.

"It was my arm," replied Arthur. "I struck it on that jagged point of rock."

"I understand," Jack answered, kindly, "but you need not be afraid. My grandmother can fix you. She's a dandy at a break."

"You do not think it's broken, surely," said Arthur in alarm.

"Well, it looks like that to me," was the cheerful answer. "I know a break any time by the way the limb is hanging."

A broken limb and no surgeon, not a boat to bring in help! Jack saw his expression of physical pain change to one of fear, and he put his arm assuringly around him.

"A break doesn't amount to much with us," he said, "you trust to me. It is not far to walk. My grandmother is the best soul in the world. So far as we know she has passed her hundredth birthday, but we don't count age, as I told you, any more than we count flowers. She'll treat you just as soft as if you were a baby. She can't talk your language but I'll stay by and translate for you."

Arthur was glad to hear it. He felt a tower of strength was near him in this broad, big-hearted fisherman.

"Now just step easily and lean on me," he went on kindly, as he almost carried him across the rocks. "Don't you get scared. It's the fear of the centipede and not the bite that puts the poison in the blood. Why, my old grandmother loves every insect. She heals the birds with broken wings and makes them fly again. She feeds even the rats out of her hands, and never yet had one to bite her."

"Is it much further?" Arthur asked. "She doesn't live up on the mountain, does she?" Somehow he placed all people of this kind up on the heights, and his courage failed him at the thought.

"She lives right here," answered Jack, stopping by a small taro patch and pond. Under a high papia tree an old bare-footed woman sat upon the grass, weaving sweet flowers into leis. She looked like one who had expected them, and her grandson smiled with pleasure that his mental "wireless" had reached her. They talked together for a time in their own tongue, then speaking English, Jack explained: "She wants you to strip to the waist and then to lie flat on your back right in the sunshine and let God's fiery finger touch your arm."

Arthur thought of the rain that had recently fallen and how from childhood they had warned him of damp grass. The woman seemed to get his thought and answered it in her own language.

"She will tell you nothing that will harm you," Jack translated. "The gentle wind has dried all Nature's tears. She can cure you quickly, but you must believe, for the medicine has ears and it has eyes."

Arthur looked at the two with horror. He could not see the deep spiritual truth lying beneath this paganism and heathen talk. Still there was nothing else he could do but follow their instruction. He would have risked almost anything for relief from a pain that was foreign, and there was no other help to be obtained.

Jack's smiling assurance gave him courage. "Trust me," he said, strongly, "and do just what we say. No harm but only good will come to you."

Arthur believed him and lay on the sun-warmed grass, while the woman skinned off the bark of a cocoanut tree above the ground where the sun struck most powerfully. Quietly and systematically she pounded it into a pulp, murmuring words he could not understand while she mixed in the salt.

"Nature heals all things," said Jack. "My grandmother knows where the most powerful medicines are. Look up and count the cocoanuts on every tree."

Arthur began to count while the long, bony fingers of the woman worked on his arm. Once or twice he was conscious of a terrific twinge, but he kept on counting harder, till the light and bright blue of the sky grew dazzling, and suddenly the cocoanuts began to tumble from the trees, play leap-frog with the sun, and then in one great heap came rolling toward him, taking the form of a man who had Jack Oahu's eyes and kindly smile, with an addition of blue sky for hair. The murmuring of Hawaiian voices came to him like the far distant sea, and he remembered no more.

Twice he awoke to feel strong fingers on his arm, adding what dimly seemed to him another coat of paint on the top of what was dry. Evening had come before the voices sounded clear.

"You are better," Jack was positively assuring him. "Wake up; you must go home."

Arthur did not feel any desire to awake. He was still deliciously drowsy and for the moment had forgotten all about his arm.

The sun was setting. The great heat of the day had gone, but the warm grass felt warm beneath him. The trees looked real again.

"It didn't hurt much, did it?" Jack continued, as he helped him to his feet. "My grandmother went into the house. She never talks after her healing. She told me to take you home and in two days remove the bandage. You will not need it after that. Your arm will be quite well. On the third morning go to greet the dawn."

Arthur listened vaguely. He was grateful for the help, but healing swift as this, seemed an impossibility.

He did not refuse Jack's offer to lean on him like a strong brother, and together they made their way towards the cottage.

"I never paid her," he said, pausing suddenly. 'What does she charge for work like this?"

Jack smiled at the idea of money mixed with their religion. "She told you you must greet the dawn," he answered. "The power from which the healing comes, the sun that shone on you while you lay there, the cocoanut that gave its bark. Go to the Source of All, she wants no money."

The tone was not meant to be reproving but Arthur felt corrected. It made his purse feel small. These people in one sense had the great idea. It was the Giver of all Good he had to thank.

He was surprised to see a crowd around the cottage. The news of the accident had traveled rapidly, and every loyal Hawaiian soul was stirred with pangs of sympathy and the desire to help. Flowers sweet and beautiful adorned his room. Fresh fish was cooking in the oven, baskets of fruit were on the table. Yee Kui had his couch prepared with books and reading lamp beside it.

"Just call on us if you are in need," said Iao, coming forward with his kindly smile. "Remember we are all your friends."

Yes, those were the right words—his friends! He looked around at the loving people full of good wishes for his happiness, ready to run and give assistance, only so sorry that there was not more that they could do.

These were the people he had shut out of his future, because they were of a different race and color. So ignorantly arrogant, fearing to step out of his narrow circle of conventional life, he had trampled on the grandest jewels, because the case which held them was not designed just like his own. He scorned his ingratitude, his bigotry and pride. How would he look if the great vision of St. John came true and all nations, kindred, people and tongues, met in the white light of universal brotherhood. Would he with a few others miss the glory of that light because he said "these people are not mine"?

He was glad to be alone in his room. In its tightly bandaged case his arm was restful, and the sense of comfort had taken the place of pain. He looked out at the sunset until the sky grew purple with the shades of night and the leaves of the samang tree had closed in sleep. Flowers in his room and loving friends around him, yet not one utterance of gratitude had he given.

A footstep sounded on the lanai. It was a step that he knew well, but tried not to expect. The scent of roses filled the room—Lilinoe was leaning through the window. Her arms were full of blossoms freshly gathered. His heart was very tender at that moment. He reached his hand to her in welcome. She raised it to her lips and he could feel her tears were falling. Tears of sympathy for his suffering. It touched his soul. Who had there ever been who had wept for him?

"I am feeling better," he said kindly, pushing his own emotion in the background. "You have been very good and thoughtful to me." He wanted to say more but it was hard to give expression.

'You will be well," she answered, gently, "but you must come and greet the dawn. On the third morning I will come for you. Be ready. You must sleep now, and sleep will make you well. Good night, Aloha."

He saw her glide away into the starlight. He did not know the meaning of her last words, nor did he know whether it was the scent of the roses which carried him out so quickly, but in another moment he was fast asleep, sleeping without a dream until the noisy call of the mynah birds aroused him like the sharp call of an alarm clock, to the sunshine of the morning.

Chapter IX

THE FISHERMAN'S STORY

Iao Hapai was fishing on the reef. The sky was full of stars. The blaze from his fagot of ti-leaves shone weirdly over the dark rocks, an enticing attraction for the unsuspecting fish. His gaze was fixed intently on the waters: the love of sport shone in his eyes. Iao had been a sportsman ever since when a little unclothed lad he had chased the fish through the waves, and cleverly caught them in his hands. He delighted in telling stories of his shark hunts and how he had sometimes come across those monsters fast asleep in the pool of a cave. His face grew brilliant and his mouth worked with excitement when he described the capture from one of the canoes, and the honor and pride he felt in dragging the man-eater home.

Lilinoe came and sat on the reef beside him. She had much on her mind that she wanted to talk to him about.

"The fish bite good tonight," he said. "I've got some fine fellows for the man who is sick. I tell you Lil, we've got to look out for that man. He can't live on flowers, however pretty they are."

"I know it," she answered.

"He wants feeding good and plenty," Iao continued. "They couldn't have got much in the land he came from. He's as thin as a streak of moonlight."

Lilinoe was watching the dancing reflection of the stars on the surface of the water.

"He's a good fellow," Iao continued, as he prepared a new bait for his hook. "What do you think of him, Lil?"

"I know that he's good, and I love him," she answered.

Iao forgot his line and fish. The live shrimp he was about to use as bait, dropped into the water and vanished from sight.

"You love him?" he said. "Why, Lil, you know nothing about him. You've had some experience with these men from the coast. You know that a love like that ends in sorrow. Don't love him, Lil. It will bring you nothing but trouble."

"How am I going to help it?" she asked.

He was for a moment baffled how to reply. He laid aside his fishing rod and sat down upon the rocks. He no longer wanted to feed the man who was sick.

"I love him," she continued, "because he brings to me something I have never had before. I love you, Iao, I love many, and within my heart and through my body, the love is warm. It beats and throbs, and I kiss you and throw my arms about you and feel you close to me, but with him, I do not need to kiss. My love for him is not that which craves the lips and arms, it is not the throbbing love which I have felt for others; it is a something that I cannot explain; it is like a light which shines into my heart so clear, so warm, so beautiful, just like the brightness of the noonday sun."

It was well that the ti-leaf had gone out, that they sat in the darkness, that she could not see the hardness that had gathered round his lips.

"When I make leis of love for you, each flower may be a kiss or an embrace, but when I make the leis for

him, each flower seems made of light, of prayer I gather
from the white rays of the sun."

"And you would marry him—this man you have only
met, and you have known us so long."

"Marry?" She seemed surprised. "Marry? No, that
could never be; not marry as we understand it, but I'm
married to him now. Love is the only marriage."

Yes, he knew that as well as she did. What would a
marriage mean with her if love did not embrace it?

"Lilinoe," he said, taking hold of her hand. "I said
this man from the coast was a mighty good fellow, and
I meant every word that I said. He may not be so fine
looking as some, but he is honest, of that I am sure. I've
talked with him lots of times on the beach. I got kind
of fond of his nature myself. He's a far better fellow than
any we've had, but I warn all the girls to watch their
steps close when it comes to those men from over the
water."

"But he's different from others," she said.

"Love always sees people different," he answered.

Lilinoe was silent. The edge of the moon looked over
the clouds like the peak of a golden mountain.

"Lilinoe," he asked suddenly, "did he encourage
you?"

"Oh, no," she responded, "that's why I love him.
Others will take all you will give them, but this man
wants nothing, not even a flower."

"But Lilinoe, he's a man from the coast," he continued. "They come over here and fall in with our life
for the time, but they won't take that life with them over
the water. It's just the fun of a day that they want. They
drink the cup of love to the dregs with our girls, and then
they go on, holding it, maybe, somewhere in memory,
but they never return. You've always been to me like

a sister. You never wanted a closer connection, but Lilinoe, you know when you make up your mind, I am ready."

"I know," she responded, "but that would not be love. You will always be just a wonderful brother, but you don't bring the music into my heart that he does. Why are you bitter, Iao? If this man only makes me glad for the time, is not it worth the sorrow that follows?"

"Not bitter," he answered, but his mouth closed tight for a moment and his expression contradicted his words. "Not bitter, Lil. The folks know here I've forgotten and forgiven the past, but it comes up again tonight with your story. You know her little grave lies at the foot of the mountain—the grave of the woman who sung in my heart like you say this man sings in yours."

Lilinoe knew her story, though he had never spoken of it in her presence.

"We people love many times, they say," he continued. "We love because we must love. That was a boyish romance and filled with all the golden glow of the early years, but it's a page cut out of my book to make way for others. I would not shut love out of my life because it had happened."

There was a pain in his voice such as she had never believed could be possible. Her emotional nature was touched.

"Tell me about it," she said.

"Maybe I will," he replied. "It may help you to hear it, though, as I said, I never think of it now. It happened before you came down from the mountain. The girl was an orphan. I'd done lots to help her and of course she grew into my heart. She was so cute and so pretty, with such saucy eyes. She would go into the water with me and catch the fish in her hands, but she never would kill them, and before I could stop her she let them go back in the waves. We were just like two kids playing together—surfing, picking shells, and making leis to twine round our necks. We climbed the mountains, we followed the sea, we went into the caves. She had the most adoring love nature and every man wanted her, but there was no other man she would look at but me. We had arranged for our marriage. The little home where I live, I built like a bird would build for her loved ones. We planned everything, and then when the time was just ready this man that you've heard of, came out from the coast.

"I really believe to this day that he loved her, though other folks say that he did not. I could not blame him for falling in love. What man could help it? I'd done it myself, but my love was honest.

"She believed he would marry her and take her over the water. She didn't know what that going over there would mean to one of her blood. She had built her world around him and didn't even realize that his people would have to live in that world. I felt her love drifting out of my heart, though I did not let on it was so. I fished and I sung and I jollied with people, and nobody thought that I knew. But the end had to come. I met them one night on the beach, with their arms around each other."

"Poor Iao," said Lilinoe, "it hurt awfully, didn't it?"

"Hurt isn't the word," he answered, intensely. "Love hurts, Lilinoe, but this had got past the hurt. It turned me to stone—it killed something in me—right there."

They were still for a moment, then he continued:

"I had the lei round my neck that I had made for her. She always wanted me to wear it first, so that all my love would go into the flowers. I delighted in making those leis. I kissed every petal and leaf as I wove them.

That night I gathered white roses. I thought they resembled her pure, white soul. Roses—whenever their scent comes to me, it carries the memory of that night and the lei.

"I made my mistake when I told her that if she wanted this fellow, to take him. Instead of doing that I ought to have acted as brother, for there was the time she needed my love and protection. But jealousy turned me insane. I let her go her own way. I had only one prayer in my heart, and that was, that all I had suffered should come back on her."

"It was natural," said Lilinoe.

"I returned to my cottage. The lei was still round my neck, but it seemed like a serpent twisting about me— strangling the life breath out of my throat. I can feel it sometimes even yet, but not as the serpent. It comes like her arms of love—clinging and asking forgiveness."

There was a long pause, then he slowly continued:

"Jack came to live with me in the cottage. The cottage I'd built for us both, with the windows looking out on the sea. Jack had the big heart, he had gone through the same. We most of us meet it—that is if we know love. He tried to make fun of it all. 'There's as good fish in the sea as ever were caught,' he would say. 'Don't stop throwing in the line because one big beauty drops into the waves.' O, I knew there was lots of fruit on the trees. I would not give in because the blossom was blighted. I held my head in the air. I was one with the girls."

"But you cared all the same," answered Lilinoe. "Did you ever meet her again?"

"Yes, once or twice, but my heart-beats were gone. I met her each time with a feeling of sorrow, for I knew what would happen. I heard she was going to marry this man. She had lost her head over him, everyone said. He had a power, no doubt, though I never could see it. He was a fine talker—his voice was gentle and soft. Give me the rough spoken man who is honest. He claimed to have what he called second vision, and he told her tales that suited her fancy, for she was always a bit of a poet. I could not talk poetry to her. I was only a man of the Islands. He went away to prepare for their wedding. He wrote several times, I believe, and then he stopped writing, and didn't come back."

"Well?" asked Lilinoe.

"Well, she went out to find him. She had heard he was in the city. She had never been out of our port, but love knows no barriers. She went out to find him. Bless her, she went out alone. It was cruel, but I could not prevent it—even though I saw the end of it all. She got to Honolulu and found the hotel from which he had written. He was not in at the time, so she sat in the lobby and waited for him. I can picture her now—just how she would look in her little pink dress. A sweet, natural flower among all the fine birds of the city. She waited until she heard the sound of his voice. It must have made her heart thrill—child of love that she was. He did not know she was there, and of course he was with another woman."

Lilinoe was earnestly listening. "And then, Iao?"

"Well, then I suppose she was struck deaf, blind and dumb, like I was on such an occasion.

"Somehow she felt she could not approach him. She crept quietly away, but wrote him a note, and begged him to see her. She waited three days for an answer. God, what those days must have been! Alone in the city—my little girl—having to beg for a word from the man who had drawn out her love.

"He would not see her, of course. He had not the courage. He sent her a note to say it was 'pau,' and that he was married."

"O, O," gasped Lilinoe. "What did she do?"

"She came back to me, but I would not receive her. I told her I could find plenty of girls."

He got up. He couldn't finish the story, but Lilinoe knew the end. She remembered the pink flowers of the vine, and the sweet scented haw that covered the grave by the mountain.

He picked up his line and baited his hook.

"I've told you all, Lil," he said, gently. "Go home and think of it."

The moon had come out, and was peeping above the mountain. Millions of stories such as this it could have written. In its bright light the two looked into each other's eyes for a moment, then, Lilinoe turned and went her way, but she did not go home, she sat on the slope of the mountain looking far out into the night.

The waves were whispering their secrets of love on the beach. The perfume of love, rose out of the flowers. Away in the distance she saw the small cottage, holy to her as a beautiful shrine. Yee Kui had just extinguished the light. Would this love bring her sorrow? Had she better crush it out of her life? How would it be possible? Could morning's hand push back the light of a golden sunrise, bursting it's way through Heaven's gate? Iao had urged her to do it. Jack, like a big strong brother, would say: "Leave it alone, Lil. Leave it alone." Out of the darkness the spirit of the broken-hearted girl seemed to rise, pointing at her the finger of warning. Her soul accepted it all for the time, but in the morning the same lei of love was found at the door of the man from the coast.

CHAPTER X
CONTEMPLATION

The woman had told Arthur to keep silent for the next few days and on the third to go and meet the dawn. They were days of rest to him. His arm was not hurting, no one disturbed him. Yee Kui only came in occasionally with some dainty or lei of sweet flowers from a nameless friend. In those two days of silence, he thought much. He was looking with straight eyes into a clear mirror, and a sense of shame was in his heart at what he saw.

It was while in these moments of concentration that the notes of Ewaliko's music reached him. They came through the clear air far in the distance like the sound of an awakening bird. The same weird sense of memory that he had experienced on the night of the luau, swept over him. He had never cared for music. The only music he had ever tolerated was the peal of the organ in the Church he had attended with his aunt. When a great musician had come to the town in which he had lived, his aunt had always attended the concert and bought a ticket for him, a ticket which generally had to be given to another because of his indisposition or unwillingness to go. He remembered how the musician's name had always been discussed by the ladies of the club, which continually met for afternoon tea in his aunt's home. He remembered how before these concerts, the worthy lady had gone to the library and refreshed her memory with the lives of musicians in the past, so that she might not be behind in her knowledge of them in any discussion in musical circles. He remembered, too, how one of the ladies, more sentimental than the others, had declared how she could close her eyes and see pictures while the musician played. He had thought at the time that this was foolish imagination, but in this boy's music, strange pictures came to him—pictures he could not understand, through which the smiling face of Lilinoe always passed.

Afraid—he would not have owned it to himself. Afraid of this strange boy who was often called a maniac—no, he was not afraid, yet, a strange nervousness overcame him as the boy stopped suddenly beside the lanai, and fixed his great dark eyes upon him. He carried in his hand a lei of pink hibiscus.

"They are warm with love," he said, as he handled their petals. "They blush with love because the sun smiles on them. Put them around your neck; you don't know how to love. You come from lands where it is cold." He laid his hand upon his heart. "You never felt it throb with love like these flowers do, only because the sun smiled on them."

He threw a lei around Arthur's neck, and without another word, was gone—his music dying in the distance like the notes of a bird that sings to the movement of its wings.

Arthur did not remove the lei when he had gone. The warmth of it—the sun-kissed flowers brought healing which he could not understand, yet, inwardly he smiled at the absurd idea of wearing flowers about his neck. He always despised the man who wore a button-hole, thought him a dandy, or one, who having no attraction in himself, sought to attract attention by a flower. The boy's words apart from his music, were ringing in his memory.

How far removed he seemed from such a love as this boy had expressed. Like the Pharisee, he had wrapped his robes of self-righteousness around him, while he gave thanks that he was not like other men. Yet, the Master to whom he prayed went down into the valley, to show the souls in darkness the way to the heights. He ate with publicans and sinners—mixed with the rabble of the street, but by the sunshine of His great and universal love, showed them the clear, white pathway to the throne of God.

He thought of a poem he had found between the pages of his Bible, only a few days before, a poem he had often read but the spirit of which he had never comprehended.

"With all thy knowledge get understanding," a wise man said. Where had his understanding been? he asked himself, as for the first time in his life, he grasped the spirit of Abou Ben Adhem, who, fearing that he did not love the Lord, asked to be written down as one who loved his fellow men. Then, he found to his surprise, that his name was placed at the head of the list of those who had declared they loved their Lord. He had never seen it in the light he saw it now. He had believed he loved his God, but had he loved his fellow man? He had always been generous with the money he possessed—he had always stretched forth his hand to help the poor and needy, he had given liberally. He remembered too, how with a long drawn sigh, one very cold winter, when the curate had been to the house with stories of poverty in the slums, his aunt had given up the thought of buying herself a new set of furs, and handed over a contribution for the starving poor instead. He remembered how her name had been head of the list of donators, and a mention of her good deeds had been given out from the pulpit. But was it love that prompted the gift—that made her long to help humanity? He could never remember any unselfish kindness being given to him, but then, how much of this unselfish kindness had he given to others? He remembered all the clubs and societies connected with the Church, which met so often in their home, under the banner of love and service. What was the subject of their conversation at those meetings after the business end was settled? Always the latest scandal, the ugly story, the stab at the one who dared to dance her life upon a broader floor than theirs. He thought of the cutting tongues and cruel condemnation in which he had joined mentally, if not by word of mouth. Yet, in love's sweet eyes, all things must be divine and beautiful. Evil could not associate itself with love. Abou Ben Adhem loved his fellowman. He saw the souls of each a spark of heavenly flame, which fanned by love, would glow into immortal fires. Again he thought of the people in high positions he had known, who had raised themselves in the eyes of the world, on a pedestal of filthy lucre—people who were admired because of this, for gold was to the multitude like light was to the moth. Were they more civilized than the savage they despised? They had been educated in the best of colleges and schools, but what had this taught them? Had it taught them that money would buy any kind of manners, therefore, it did not matter how they acted, because their title was there, their estate was there, their bank-books were there, and these passports would allow them to push to the wall the one who was empty-handed, would allow them to draw in their evening gowns to avoid the contamination of those who did not possess such things—or, had it taught them the highest of all lessons, that a man of a faultless character needs no prop behind him, no brazen trumpet in front—he can pass through the world unshod, and always be received like a prince?

He thought of those living in a narrow little space, cased in with golden walls, slamming the door in the face of worth, unless it came with a chain of gold; and then he thought when the great eruption descended, what would those golden walls avail them? He saw life like a broad stretch of sand, and humanity like children building castles there; some of the sturdiest, though not always the most gifted, built them high and strong, and ascending to the top, looked down on those below. But the rain came and washed away the castles—the short lived triumph was over, and all were together upon the sands again. So when pedestals crumbled to ashes and gold melted into the stream and palaces decayed, and when they stood disrobed of all but the immortal soul; when earthly pomp was accounted nothing, where would they find ther footing? Kingdoms shattered, thrones fallen, kings, queens, emperors, side by side with the man of the street—then why all this division? why all this sect and nation against nation—brothers and sisters of the same needs, the same hearts and souls—all hearts beating as one, united by the love of God. He closed his eyes. A prayer for the realization of such a love as this, rose from his starved and lonely heart.

Chapter XI

THE WANAAO

The stars were shining above Kaihakala's heights, shining like golden tapers over a mighty cathedral, when on the third morning after his accident, Arthur was awakened by Lilinoe's footsteps and her soft voice calling him to come and meet the dawn.

He removed the bandage from his arm before he dressed, bathed it in warm water, and was surprised to feel the use of it again. As he swung it backwards and forwards, he smiled to himself at what he called the innocence of those dear good people, he had found himself amongst. He imagined how the surgeon would have laughed at such a quick recovery from a break. There was not a mark on the arm, nor the sign of a bruise, nothing to tell it had been injured in any way, and yet that good fisherman, so honest and so true, had made him believe the arm was broken, and the kind old Hawaiian woman had chanted a prayer over him, while she bound it up with some strange concoctions, about which he knew nothing. He had really believed himself that he was badly injured, and he could not grasp the meaning of a recovery so quick. Of course the fall had shaken his nerves, that was true, but then he remembered the kindness of these dear people, and he must try and return it by falling in with their beliefs and superstitions at this time.

A soft cool wind blew through the branches of the iron-wood pines, carrying a delicious fragrance towards him, when he opened his door and stepped out on the lanai.

The girl awaited him with her finger on her lips. There was something so sacred in that morning silence broken only by the music of the distant sea—something so sweet and so mysterious, that he was glad he did not need to talk.

He followed her over the dew-wet grass, moving as one moves through the enchantment of a lovely dream. He did not ask where they were going. He was conscious of a great happiness, a rest from fear, a light within, such as his darkened soul had never known. He knew that this was not connected with the girl—but in the unseen, where all God's gifts are awaiting our acceptance, he had touched something more glorious than earthly wealth could buy.

They followed the road in silence for some time, then Lilinoe stopped and grasped his hand. "Hush!" she intensely whispered. "The Wanaao!" The darkness was slowly breaking round them like a fading mist. The trees stepped forth from chaos and outlined their lovely forms against the sky. On every side the mighty cliffs guarding the sea lifted their heads aloft. The scent of awakening flowers came riding towards them on the air. Out of the soft wet grass the tiny faces of the honohonos began to shine forth like Heaven tinged drops of dew: then suddenly in one unbroken chain of song, the voices of a thousand wakening birds broke forth in ecstasy of praise.

Arthur was about to speak, but Lilinoe lifted her hand for silence.

"Wait," she whispered again, as one would whisper on ground that was sacred, "the second dawn!"

The light was growing brighter in the East. The trees were whispering greeting to each other. The scattered clouds became a blaze of fire. Rays of primrose painted themselves across the sky, making the great branches of the palms look black by vivid contrast. A sudden wind blew strongly from the sea, shaking out nature's garments in her morning call, whispering mysteriously through hidden caves, joining her voice with waves and water-falls and songs of birds. Then clear and beautiful like the face of an angel smiling through a frame of gold, the sun shone forth in splendor, throwing aside the curtains of the dawn, donning brightest robes, blazing a trail across the waters, and enfolding the whole Island in the warm embrace of great healing love.

Lilinoe lifted her arms and eyes in blessing. She turned to the North, the South, the East and the West. She sent out her call to the gods of the sea and the wind. She gathered the power from the four corners of the earth. Power for the weak, health for the sick, youth for the aged, and life for the dying.

Arthur stood spellbound while he listened. His whole being was responding to the gathered force, as the flowers were responding to the sun. He looked from right to left at the splendor of the scene. They stood on the massive rock overhanging the sparkling sea. The waves were curling inwards, lovingly touching the sand. Over the glistening leaves of the fields of sugar cane, rose massive banks of ferns and flowers, trailing vines through which shining waterfalls, catching the glory of the morning light, became transformed to rainbows of fire.

Lifted out of himself by a force that almost overwhelmed him, he looked towards Lilinoe. She had for the time forgotten his presence. Unconscious of her beauty she was transfigured by power. Wrapped in the golden light of the morning she stood with the lei of flowers on her hair—flowers which seemed to have absorbed every color of the sunrise right into the center of their being. As he watched her bow to the earth in rapturous adoration, a current strong as electricity swept over him. It was startling in its sudden force. In moments like these we make our great at-one-ment. It may be that we only touch the robe, but even when yet a great way off, eternal love comes forth to meet us.

She left him suddenly and walked to where the bell-flowers swung snow white, and on the vines the pink and purple kowali grew. She began to break away the leaves and fill her hands with the flowers. She went on her way without looking back, and he felt he need not follow. He remained on the rocks until the light grew too dazzling for his eyes, then slowly he returned under the quiet shade of loving trees, cool and restful as the gentle clouds which pass over a dazzling sun. He wanted to be alone— to hold the splendor of the morning to his soul. He wanted to draw a fence around this picture, and to hang it in the frame of memory where he might look on it forever. In such a world as this he had never until now opened the door to glories unrevealed. For twenty-five years he had been an invalid—starved in the land of plenty—hungered outside his father's gates while love's dear hand was on the latch longing to let him in.

* * *

Next day it rained heavily. Looking out on the drenched landscape and sunless sky, Arthur found it almost impossible to believe that the scene of desolation was the gorgeous one of the day before. His spirits corresponded with the weather. No longer on the crest of the wave, he dropped suddenly from the elevation he had touched. He sat silent on the lanai, longing for he knew not what. He felt as if the experience of the day before had all been a dream. The foot-lights had gone from the transformation, and only the mist remained.

He assured himself he was glad Lilinoe had not come to see him, but the day was long and irksome, and when night came he retired early, hoping sleep would come as easily as it had been doing these last few days. He didn't know whether he had slept or not, he would have taken the negative side of such a question, had he been asked, and would have declared he had never even closed his eyes, but he was suddenly aroused in the same way as he had been his first night on the beach. The same sense of horror with the nervous chill, had seized him. Where was he, what was that noise? It was too near the house to be the waves of the sea, and yet it came with the same terrific roar. Could it be rain—yes, beating violent rain, which threw itself against the house with the force of an invisible army. The wind was blowing a hurricane, and away in the distance came the smashing of waves against rocks and shore. He reached out his hand for a light, when the house swayed backwards and forwards, like a ship at sea. He shouted for Yee Kui. Immediately the door opened and the little Chinaman appeared.

"Why did you not come before?" he asked with more warmth of temper than he had believed himself capable of.

"I wait for master's move," Yee Kui answered, as he straightened the candle which had bent and been adjusted many times in the heat.

"What does all this mean?" he began, almost blaming the Chinaman for both storm and earthquake.

"Mountains takee walkee," he said smiling. His cool poise was aggravating. Did nothing disturb him? Was he just an automatic machine?

"Don't you hear the rain?" he asked.

"Rain verree goodee—makee flowers grow." He was walking round the room quietly picking up and adjusting the things which the quake had displaced. The storm continued to beat. "Madame Pele verree sore to-night," he said.

"Madame Pele! what are you talking of, Yee Kui?" Arthur asked, believing that the sense of the man had quite forsaken him.

"Madame Pele live in big volcano on the other island. When the people don't treat her well she rakes fire and sends the storms."

"I gave you credit for more sense, Yee Kui," Arthur said. "How can you believe such rubbish—that an imaginary goddess living in the depths of a pit of flame could influence the weather, and send destruction on the Island."

Yee Kui continued to pick up the fallen things from the floor and return them to their places, and to bail out the water which was coming through windows and doors. Arthur lifted the blind for a moment, when a brilliant flash of pink lightning made him drop it just as quickly.

"I don't want any more of this," he said, as if Yee Kui had the power to stop the elements. "If this continues, the whole island is liable to be washed into the sea."

The Chinaman smiled at the prospect.

"Then we all wash away together," he replied. "No one left lonely by himself. I go with Master to another world."

Arthur was silent. The words were almost a reproach. The fearlessness of the Chinaman might come through the fatalistic belief of his race, that nothing happened by chance, and what had to be would be, but it brought to

Arthur the memory of what he had always been taught
—nothing could happen without the will of God. What
the Chinaman's beliefs in the hereafter were, he didn't
know, but his absolute confidence in facing it—was a
tonic.

"You are very brave, Yee Kui," he said quietly.

"I see worse storms than this on Yangtzee River,"
Yee Kui answered. "Big storms, whirlpools, rapids,
swallow up the little sampans. Master got good house
to live in. Gods love master verree much."

Though he coupled other gods with the One God,
yet, his very words were comforting to Arthur. If God
loved His children, as he believed He did, surely under
all conditions they were safe.

"You may go now, Yee Kui," he said quietly. "You
need your rest and the storm is settling down."

Yee Kui placed the candle nearer to him, then with
a bow, repeated the assurance as he went through the
door—"Master sleepee verree well."

Chapter XII

CONFESSIONS

The morning light broke up the storm. The rain now fell in soft and gentle showers, and Arthur sat by the window of his cottage, weary after his wakeful night. Though he would not have acknowledged it even to himself, he was watching for Lilinoe, and he felt a sudden thrill of joy when he saw her come running barefoot, bare-headed through the shower towards him.

"Why don't you come out and enjoy yourself?" she asked, shaking the wet drops from her abundant curly hair. "It's too close in the house and too depressing. Come out—let's have the fun with nature we had when we met the dawn."

"That was different," he replied, "the weather was beautiful then."

"It's just as beautiful now, she answered.

"O, no, it's not," he contradicted, "the rain is miserable and cold; such heavy rain, it comes down like a cloudburst. They talk of a roaring wind, and a roaring fire, but the same comparison would suit this rain."

She laughed merrily, "Come out and get drenched," she said. "Look at the flowers, the rain will put new varnish on their coats, and make them grow."

He never knew just how to take her, her change of moods was as aggravating as the climate.

"You forget that I am sick," he said.

She looked at him with mischief twinkling in her eyes. "Oh, no, you are not," she answered, "you went to greet the dawn."

The memory of it made his face look brighter.

"The rain is over now," she said. "It never lasts for long. Look at the sunshine."

The clouds had parted suddenly. Patches of blue sky appeared between them. Long silvery shafts of light descended downwards. "Come out," she said again, "come out on the lanai, let us talk."

Her tone was irresistible. He knew she would not come into the house, this child of nature and the out of doors. How wonderful to be so free. No fear of colds nor change of weather, growing with rains and storms and sunshine. He went and joined her on the lanai.

"Let's watch the change of scene," she said. "The sun is building a new world out of the old."

"Making a new picture out of the same canvas," he replied. "Look at those drifting clouds, would you believe a storm could pass so quickly?"

"As quickly as your mood," she answered. "You were so sad and so despondent. Why should we feel unhappy in this lovely world?"

"Yes, why?" he questioned, as he looked across the scene in front of him, where brightened into splendor by the storm, the colors flashed like poems written by an angel's pen of gold. "Why art thou cast down?" the Psalmist asked his soul, and he was facing himself with the question put forth centuries ago.

"In one way," he said at last, "we are ungrateful mortals. To a certain extent you people of the Islands seem to have a greater conception of happiness."

"We live and love," she answered. "That's all there is to do, and so we are happy."

"The God love is everything," he responded, "but the human love will bring you pain."

"I know it," she declared, "but even so, we would rather have the pain than not have love."

He did not answer, his eyes were looking absently on the huge mynah birds walking the long leaves of the banana trees, sunning their wet feathers in the returning warmth.

"You have such lots to love," she went on. "You must have loved so many times."

Had he? Again he saw his narrow, limited life as he had seen it the other day. He flushed slightly but threw off the embarrassment and met her on her own ground.

"Pray, what about yourself?" he asked.

Her merry laugh rang out, gladdening the heart of Yee Kui over his cooking in the kitchen. It was the laugh of love—the laugh of memory.

"O, I've loved often," she replied, "but not as I love you."

Had a thunder bolt fallen at his feet, Arthur could not have been more startled. Love him! It brought the blood surging to his face—this frank confession. He did not know exactly how to meet it, and he was glad when she continued:

"I know we must seem strange to you, but we're just people of the Islands, and if we love, we have to tell it—it hurts too badly if we don't."

One of the natives passed while she was speaking. He called out a cheerful Aloha, and showed his well-set teeth in a happy smile.

"Aloha!" she called. "Where are you going?"

"By the boat," he answered gaily. "My wife she found another man. I go Honolulu."

He went laughing on his way, twanging his ukelele and her glad laugh joined with his.

So that was their idea of marriage! She answered his shocked look with words that shocked him more.

"He is happy," she said gladly, "and his wife is happy too. She found another love, and maybe he did, or he wouldn't be so glad. They both go to their love, and it is very beautiful."

"Beautiful?—a desecration of the marriage law?"

"It is no desecration—the law is love, and if there is no love there is no law."

"You talk at random," he replied. "You do not understand the sacredness of marriage."

"Do you understand it?" she spoke as one who asked for knowledge.

He hesitated before he made reply. "The promise is to have and hold."

"To hold?"—she looked at him in perplexity. "To hold that glorious thing that we call love? We do not need to hold it. That would show fear, and love is free. If I did not love a man, he could not make me love him just because he held me by his side."

"Then, you mean to say that man is right to rejoice because his wife's love left him for another?"

"If he loved her, he would want her to be happy. If he did not love her, he would be glad for her to go." She was laughing at his seriousness.

"Hush!" said Arthur, in a conventional whisper. You must not be so free. Someone might hear what you were saying."

"Why should we care?" she asked. "You white people are always so afraid, and want to keep these things a secret. Love should not be a secret. A secret is a thing of shame. The sun blazes its love story on the earth. If it did not love the flowers they would not live. The birds sing out sometimes as if their throats would break. If they did not love their lives they would not sing. Love is so beautiful—they want to give the world some of its power. Everything loves, or nothing would be living. If I love you, why should I crush it back until my heart is bursting? Love has to give expression. You may not love me, Arthur, but you never can prevent me loving you."

She spoke his name unconsciously, the name by which she always called him in her soul. It sounded pretty on her lips. He listened in amazement. He thought how his aunt's back would have stiffened had she known of this. What food for conversation it would have furnished among the ladies in the drawing-room of their home. He recalled one story rooted deeply in his mind by its constant repetition, the story of a girl who had written the confession of her love to the man who idealized by distance, had made the sunrise of her life. He remembered how he had figuratively patted that man on the back when he heard that he had returned her letter, declaring it was incomprehensible to him. No doubt it was—for love's eyes must be very deep to comprehend the vastness of its purity.

"When you have gone away," she went on slowly— (Those words relieved his mind. She knew then he would have to go. A sudden fear had filled his soul, that she might want to claim him then and there.) "When you have gone away, I shan't forget you. I won't want any other man. I'll send my leis of love to you in thought across the sea, and when the stars come out I'll sit upon the rocks where I first met you. I'll ask the gods each night to bless you—when you have gone away."

Her eyes were full of poetry. It was her tone more than her words that struck his heart.

When he had gone away! Yes, gone to what? He shuddered when he thought of any other land. When he thought of crossing the big, lonely waters, and meeting none on the other side. He saw the long, bleak, empty road in front of him—loveless—companionless—*when he had gone away.*

Almost unconsciously he reached his hands toward her, and caught hers tightly in his own.

"I am not going away yet, Lilinoe," he said, gently. "Don't let us speak of that. You say I have so many to love me—well, not so many but what I can appreciate your love. You have said right. Without love the flowers would not smile, the birds would not sing—the world would not be—and without love, how could we find God?"

She came and sat down at his feet, clasping her hands on his.

"You know so much," she said. "I know so little. If I could find your God, maybe I would know more."

If she could find his God. What had he done to help her find Him? He had hugged his religion closely to his heart. No wonder it had given him so little comfort—when he had not shared it with another.

"Did you never read the Bible, Lilinoe?" he asked.

"O, no,"—"I never read. My mother said I learnt it quickly, but I never wanted books. Why do we need to read, when it's all here?" She pointed to a thousand stories written in the colors of the sun-bathed land—in the mighty cliffs, and in the palms where the cocoanuts grew. "I guess the gods have given us enough; we don't need books." She said.

"Why do you talk of different gods?" he asked. "There is only one, who said, 'Thou shalt have no other before me.' "

He passed the Bible to her as he spoke, but she shook her head.

"Don't ask me to read that," she said. "It's too big and thick—it would take me far too long to understand."

She saw the look of disappointment on his face, and added:

"You tell me all about it. I love to hear you talk."

He had never talked religion, even to his aunt, although she had always spoken of him as a good Christian boy. Her words were ringing in his ears now. If he were Christian, then he ought to give light to the darkness of this girl.

She was sitting at his feet in expectation. Her eyes were riveted upon him. He cleared his throat and then repeated, "There is one God, and He knows all. All things belong to Him."

He opened the Bible while he spoke, and began in a dull monotone to read the story of creation.

The girl listened, as she would have listened to one of the old legends of the Islands. Listened with mouth agape at the rapidity of movement. Her vivid imagination following closely the quick work of His hand until the seventh day was reached, and Arthur paused and looked up as he said "and God rested on the seventh day from His work."

"He'd need to," she cried in amazement. "I never heard of any work so quick. It beats the menahunes we think so wonderful. They were the fairies who built up a temple in the night—little bits of fellows just the length of my hand. They lived in the woods and hid in the caves; they slept among the trees and between the ferns.

When we were children we used to look for them among the bell flowers. My, but this must have been a wonderful man to work faster than they worked and nobody to help him. What did he make after He'd rested?"

"He made man in His own image."

She was silent a moment, regarding him in wonder. "You mean He made all men to look like Him? but they don't look like Him now, do they? Some men are handsome, and some are not; some men are old and some are sick."

"There was only one who really kept the likeness, and that one was His Son."

"Had He a Son? What was His name?"

Arthur turned over the pages of the Bible and slowly read—"His name shall be called Wonderful, Counsellor, Mighty God, the Everlasting Father, the Prince of Peace."

She repeated each word after him, and shook her head. "What did they give Him so many names for?" she asked. "How could they remember them all? Hadn't they got a shorter one that they could call Him by—a nickname?"

He knew she didn't mean it for sacrilege, so there was no reproof in his voice, as he said "they shall call His name Jesus, for He shall save His people from their sins."

"Jesus—I like that," she answered, as her musical voice slowly repeated and lingered on the word. "I'll call Him Jesus, it's easier to remember than all those other names. Save His people from their sins—their sins—" she repeated. "That means sickness, doesn't it?"

"Sickness is not a sin," he answered.

"The old Hawaiians used to say it was," she said.

"There was a time when no one was sick, but everyone was happy, and we lived forever. Often in dreams I see that time. I see our island as it was, no sorrow and no pain. I believe it will come true, this beautiful dream that comes to me in the deep sleep of the night and sometimes in the early morning. I told it once to the Kahuna; he could interpret dreams, and he asked me what sleep I saw it in, and I told him in the sleep before the dawn, and again in the deep sleep of the night, and he said it was not a dream of the past, but a dream of something yet to come. Some day we will have such a land, I know it, for the angels of the dawn have told it to me."

Arthur was silent a moment, then he said "sickness is sent from God to draw man nearer to him."

"I should think they could draw nearer if they were not sick, when folks get sick they seem to lose their mind, nothing looks pretty to them. Do all people everywhere know all about this God, does all the world except us on this little island, away from everyone, but just ourselves, know all about this one who made life beautiful for everyone—do they know, Arthur? They cannot know, for I have heard them say that across the waters people are sick and poor, and they fight to get things from each other. O, they can't know all that you have told me, or how could they be sick, or poor or sad, when He made them all to look like Him, and even if they did get sick, couldn't He make them well?"

"He sent His Son into the world to heal them," Arthur answered.

"To heal them? then why didn't He heal you?"

Arthur paused again. Her question had struck right home, He was talking of the healing Christ, yet she had reminded him that he himself was sick.

"That was two thousand years ago," he answered.

"O—" there was a world of pathos in her tone. "If it's two thousand years ago, I don't want to hear about it. I want some one who can heal the sick now."

They were silent for a moment. Then a long drawn sobbing sigh broke from her lips. Her head dropped on her lap, her whole frame shook and her tears fell like rain from clouds long charged.

"Why do you cry?" he asked, stirred to emotion by the intensity of her sobs.

"Because there's no one who can heal the sick," she said. "They're all dead, every one of them."

"But Christ still lives," he answered, with a power that surprised him.

A gleam of hope like sunshine in a storm, lit up her face. The consciousness of life, so strong in the Hawaiians made it quite possible to believe that those who knew it's secret, as the ancients, could be upon the earth plane for two thousand years. Still, doubt was in her mind with the question:

"Why did He never make you well if He still lives, why don't you go to Him and let Him heal you?"

"I do not know," he answered slowly. "Maybe, I'm too far away."

A cool wind made him shiver slightly, and with her usual thought, she took the shawl from the back of his chair and bound it round his limbs.

"I know the gods can live forever," she said gently. "And if He lives—" She paused a moment, looked around and came a little closer. "I have something I would like to tell you," she continued. "No one knows, except, I sometimes think Ewaliko, though he never breathed it to me, but he listens for the voices in the night time, and the spirits of the wind have carried it to him. I have a brother, the one I told you about, by sole companion of

the mountains, the child my father and mother loved,
and—that brother is a leper." Arthur recalled the stories
of the leper islands and immediately imagined he was
there. She did not give him time to question, but
continued:

"I told you how we lived up on the mountain—how
happy we were in our little home. Akana always loved
me dearly. We never quarreled like some children. We
went laughing, hand in hand, through life without a
care. But when our father and our mother left us he felt
lonely, and he begged to come down here to live. I did
not want to come. I felt nearer to my dear ones on the
mountains—it seemed as if the angels walked with me
upon the heights. I loved our little home where we had
planted our garden, so near to the sunrise and the sunsets,
and the rainbows—but I came down for his sake—and
because it made him happy, I was satisfied to stay. Boats
came in once a week, bringing girls from the coast. A
few came for the day with fancy things to sell, and went
back the next morning. One of them stayed a week. She
had blue eyes and golden hair. Akana had not met a
woman with blue eyes. He never ceased to look at her—
he called her his sweet goddess of the dawn, he wept
when she set sail, and then of course he followed her to
Honolulu. I did not try to prevent him, He would have
been unhappy, and I wanted him to feel that he was free.
I watched the waves for his return. He never wrote—
but I heard of him from men who came from Honolulu.
They told me he was happy and that he was king of the
beach at Waikiki—and everybody loved him. He was so
tall, so strong, so handsome, and so kind. He taught
the girls to surf-board and to play the ukulele. He went
with them on hikes, and made the leis, and garlanded
them with flowers. For seven long years he kept away,

but I always knew he would return. I kept our little home for him up on the mountain—kept his canoe and all his little treasures—and one day he came back."

She stopped and laid her hand on Arthur's arm.

"How he got back I never knew, but every foot of the ground was known by him. He knew the underground routes no other man could travel. He came back to me by night, for they were hounding him. He came back— but he was *a leper.*"

She stopped again—so long this time that Arthur said: "Go on. I'll try to help you."

"And then I hid him," she continued. I hid him where no other man could find his whereabouts. I knew the secret hiding places of the past—the old Kahunas had shown them to me, for they had hidden many in the times of war. They came to seek him from the other Island, but when they heard no man had landed from the boats they went their way. He scarcely had a stain or blemish, but they had branded him a leper. They wanted to take him to the Island where the men are like rotting leaves. Take Akana—my lovely brother—as strong and beautiful as the Hawaiian gods. I have hidden him until he gets his healing. There is a certain flower that grows high on the mountains—and it was shown to me one night in dreams. A flower like the one I gave you the time we met. You wondered why it did not die. It only dies shedding its blood for others. It could not die another way. It is the flower of life, and holds within its petals the lifeblood of a man who offered all he had in service."

"I remember," Arthur said. "There was something almost uncanny in that flower. It lived so long it frightened me. Sometimes I seemed to see it shining in the darkness, like a blood-red star."

"I always find it by its light," she answered, "dear little flower—it gives its life for love."

"It is a pretty legend," he responded, "but how can its life help your brother?"

"He crushes the oil out of its roots and rubs it on his scars. Each drop is drawn like lifeblood from its petals —all color leaves them, and they fall away and die."

"And is it helping him?"

"It must be, no life that gave itself for love could be in vain."

That moment Arthur longed to find expression. He longed to tell her of that life of love and service, about which mentally he had known so long—but the soul consciousness of which, like the starved prodigal, was yet a great way off.

She was kneeling in the attitude of prayer. Her strong appeal made him feel wretched.

"How can I reach this One you tell about?" she asked. "How can I get His help to heal my brother?"

"Believe on Him," was all that he could say.

"Do you believe?"

"Of course I do"

"But yet you say that you are sick. Why did He never make *you* well?"

He could not answer her. The *why* was standing out before him.

"There are many things we can't explain," he said, "but if you read this book, which is His life, you will know all."

He had never felt so helpless, so ashamed. This girl whom he had thought the heathen of the Islands, was asking questions that he could not meet.

He laid the Bible on her lap and opened it at the New Testament. "Read the life of Jesus as it was on earth," he said.

She seemed more interested and glanced down at the pages. Perhaps it was the vibration of the concentrated power that reached her, for she got up suddenly and without a word, went on her way, holding it close to her heart.

Arthur followed her with a prayer. She was a heathen, he believed, and maybe the reason why God had brought him here, was not to get his health, but to bring light into her darkness.

CHAPTER XIII

THE SOUL'S AWAKENING

Lilinoe found a quiet corner on the rocks, and eagerly began to read the testament. To her the story known so well by him came with the freshness of a beautiful romance. With lively imagination she followed the pictures as vividly as if they had been flashed upon the screen. She saw in her surrounding on the beach, the little town where the young virgin lived. Mary must have felt the angels round her many times, and maybe heard the flutter of their wings: but, oh, the glorious astonishment to have one come into her home—to talk with one, and hear the message of her coming motherhood. That God was sending her a child whose name should be called "Wonderful—Counsellor—The Mighty God—The everlasting Father—The Prince of Peace—who would rise over the world like a shining star and of whose kingdom there should be no end."

O, marvelous gift of love. Love which made angels sing with joy! In imagination she was carried away to the hills of Bethlehem, where in the calmness of the night the shepherds watched their flocks. Out of the star-strewn darkness she saw the light break like the golden sunrise—bursting the gates of Heaven apart—bearing the soul to earth upon the brilliance of its rays.

The picture stepped forth vividly before her. Faces of angels smiled out of the sunset. Into her heart the joyous message of glad tidings crept—warm, overpowering, beautiful. She had to pause for a few moments—the glory of it was so great.

The colors in the sky began to fade. The waves washed up the sand and wet her feet, but she did not notice, only when one more powerful than the others splashed heavily across her lap, she receded a little—but still continued to read.

The shining moon came up like a silver lamp. She walked towards her home, still reading, lighted her candle and sat down on the bed. Each character was alive to her, and found its double on the Island. In the old man Simeon, who had waited for the consolation of Israel, and to whom it had been revealed that he should not see death until he had seen the Lord Christ, she pictured the old Kahuna who had freed her from her bondage when a baby, especially when led by the spirit into the temple he took the child in his arms, and spoke the beautiful prophecy for the future.

The old prophetess Anna, who lived in the temple and served God with fasting and with prayer, was just as real to her. Was not Jack's grandmother the same? Did she not live on fruit and flowers and spend her time in praying for the sick?

In the fishermen who left their nets in response to the call of the Great Teacher she saw the strong Hawaiians of the beach. The care-free life in the open, appealed to her. How beautiful to walk with Him among the corn —or to sit in the ship by the blue waters of the lake, and listen to His stories of field flowers that lived without a worry for tomorrow, and yet wore robs more gorgeous than a king's. He belonged to her right away. He was a part of her Island. He was moving in their midst. She went with Him up on the mountains, where He withdrew to be alone with the great power. How well she understood the rest and peace He must have felt, drawing so close to God in the great silence of the heights. One after another she followed the healings. She saw the darkness of obsessing forces pass away. She felt the touch upon her eyes like human fingers when the blind received their sight.

He cleansed the leper. She could not see the page for tears. He even raised the dead—and at the sunset hour, all came to Him, and all were healed.

The wick of the candle fell and the light went out, but she did not regret it. Heavy, black clouds were banked before the moon, but her room was full of the golden glow which she had carried from the pages.

She placed the Bible underneath her cheek and dropped down on the pillow.

He healed them every one. He cleansed the leper. All was well. She had left her brother with Him in the sunset, and the eyes of love were fixed on him.

* * *

Next morning Arthur missed Lilinoe from the beach. She had gone up the mountain to read. Heights of silence, birds and flowers, fig trees and palms—were surely a fitting background for her story. Her whole soul was absorbed in the short but graphic description of the storm at sea. She had known so many of those storms —storms that rose out of nothingness, sweeping across the Island like the sudden anger of a giant roused from sleep. She saw the waves come up like mountains and throw themselves against the frail and trembling ship. Above the gale she heard the wild and agonizing cry of the disciples: "Lord, save us, or we perish."

Would He awaken to their need—He who had saved so many? Out of the wildness of the storm a voice was speaking. The wind was listening to its power. The waves, like armies weary of a fight, fell thankfully to rest. Darkness was rolled away by dawn's white hand— and like a sea gull floating homeward, she saw the ship with dripping sails glide to the shore.

Then there was nothing impossible for Him to do. A field undreamed of opened to her in the promise, "Whatsoever ye shall ask in my name, that will I give unto you." He had said, "Whatsoever." She could ask for anything. The world was built anew.

The reality of this grew stronger when she came to the prayer pulsating with the power of ages, "Our Father." She read it many times. She claimed her unity with divinity at once. The gods that she had known were far away. They existed in the Heavens and ruled the earth and seas. She had called on them as mighty gods, but not one would she have dared to approach with that name which represented love. "Our Father." "Our Father." She repeated it again. She looked out over the beautiful Island, shining like a many colored jewel in the light. She saw men working in the fields of sugar cane— hoers and tillers of the ground. Down at the wharf where the weekly boat had just come in, strong young Hawaiians lifted and unloaded heavy freight. The fishermen were throwing in their nets and wading out into the sea. A little Jap mother toiled up the dusty hill with a baby on her hip and three small children clinging to her skirts. The Chinese cook was standing in the doorway of the small shack which represented restaurant and hotel. All these were given the right to call Him Father, and approach Him as a God of love.

"Which art in Heaven."

She had known of that beautiful region they called "Wakea," where she believed her loved ones were. She had got the glimpse of it in visions—but this new Heaven was not so far away. She drew it with the warm blue sky around her—this Heaven of love in which the Father dwelt.

"Hallowed be Thy name."

She bowed her head in holy reverence. She paused as one might do on sacred ground—for the power of that great name had dawned upon her in the "Whatsoever ye shall ask in my name."

"Thy Kingdom come."

His Kingdom. The Kingdom of a God of Love. What would it mean if such a kingdom came? It would mean there would be no more war, for Love could never fight it's brother. It would mean there would be no more sickness, for Love could never see it's loved one suffer. No beating tempests, and no storms at sea. No quarrelling, no jealousy, no striving for the bigger gain, no cruelties, no unkind words. His kingdom—the kingdom of such a God, and over all He would be King. How she would love to serve Him, even if only to wash His feet with tears of love.

"Thy will be done on earth, as it is done in Heaven."

How easy to do the will of Love, since whatsoever Love designed must only be for good. Earth and Heaven would then become as one, united like the colors in a sunrise.

"Give us this day our daily bread."

Want she had never known in this sweet land, where fruit bore down the trees, and streams and waterfalls refreshed the thirst, where plenty wrote itself on every side. She only need stretch forth her hand and the supply was there. Did this mean food of any other kind? she questioned. Were these souls hungering for the truths this Book was giving her? Why had she not heard of it before? Why did not the whole world know that it might hunger and thirst no more, but might daily be refreshed by this sweet spiritual food.

"And forgive us our trespasses."

She said the words like a repentant child, for in the sight of Love she must have erred a thousand times, but had just as quickly been forgiven.

"As we forgive them that trespass against us."

Her eyes became suffused with tears. Her mind went to the lonely cave, the walls of which were hiding one she held so dear. She thought of all that he had borne from men of other races. Men who were jealous of his strength and power. Men, who envying his care-free spirit, kind, unselfish ways, and winning personality, had torn his heart to pieces by their cruelty. Mocked at his colored blood—trampled his soul beneath their feet—and thankful at last to find a spot to which they could point, were rejoicing now to know the hounds were on his track.

Could she forgive them? Through ages past the voice of love eternal whispered to her soul, "They know not what they do."

"And lead us not into temptation, but deliver us from evil."

She had been taught to believe in evil forces—wandering souls, which had the power to follow and to torture, which came in the darkness of the night and often in the daytime. She thought of those who had been prayed to death—good people—some of them,—but with no power to resist. She remembered one young girl who had rushed to her for refuge. Her jealous lover had gone to the praying men to have her prayed out of the body, sooner than see her married to another man. She saw again the terrified eyes and the trembling hands as she

watched for the coming of the darkness—knowing that
when the first star blinked, her end had come.

She remembered how she too had felt the force sent
out—and how helpless she was to ward it off. The girl
had died before the darkness fell. O, had she known of
this great God of Love she would have broken every other
power by the white magic of "Deliver us from evil."

A thrill of joy went through her at the positive end
of the prayer.

"For Thine is the kingdom, and the power, and the
glory—*forever and ever.*"

Then there was no doubt about it. His kingdom—
His power—His glory, remained with them always—
forever and forever. She raised her eyes—rested her el-
bows on her knees, and dropped her chin upon her hands.

Her reverie was broken by the sound of gentle music,
coming like notes of birds through distant trees. Ewaliko
was walking towards her. His sensitive nature had
touched the power, and he came like a little child, and
sat down on the grass at her feet. She took his hand in
hers and gazed into his eyes.

"Ewaliko, I have found something beautiful," she
said. He looked at the Bible lying on the grass. He
could see the aura shining round it like rays from a golden
sun.

"I know," he answered, slowly. 'I found that jewel
long ago—but it's too bright for me to wear."

He laid his head down on her lap just like a tired baby.
"I don't need another sunrise, when you are here to shine
on me," he said.

Her hands played with his curly hair, like the hands
of a strong and loving mother. "But, Ewaliko," she said,
gently, "this is a sunrise you have never seen, this sun
arises in the heart."

He smiled, but quickly grasped her meaning. "Then I should never feel the cold nor see the darkness."

"No," she responded, in a voice of triumph, "there could be no more darkness for you—where light forever shines."

She knew he was resting—for his features often so distraught with fear were calm and still. It was a joyous thought that she need worry over him no more. She need not try to keep him on the mountain and watch to see if all were kind to him. He was protected by a God of love, who would deliver him from evil. He got her thought—he raised his head—his eyes smiled into hers again.

"I know," he said. "I know there's One who walks in that bright light. Sometimes when I am very still He comes and speaks right through my music. Sometimes He talks with me. He always comes when I'm most lonely. I lose Him in the crowd down there. I cannot even hear the rustle of His garments. Some time, maybe, I'll see His face."

He walked away while he was speaking, taking the fern strewn path through falling clouds which dropped on every side of him like sun-tipped wings of guardian angels.

* * *

The day wore on. Lilinoe did not need to eat. Like the woman of Samaria, she had forgotten the well from which she had been drawing. Time and again she paused, the power had grown so great. Her whole soul filled with rapture. She loved Him, this strong and wonderful man. She felt His presence close beside her. She saw Him clothed in all His beauty, magnificent in strength and courage, and yet so full of love and tenderness that He could weep in sympathy with those who wept. She reached forth her hand as she thought of the woman who touched the hem of His garment. A thrill passed through her, such as the woman must have felt when she was healed. Would He have entered their little grass hut, had He come to their island? He entered the homes of others, and oh, how changed those homes must have been because His dear feet entered there. What a strength and power there must have been over all who followed in His foot-steps, and He still lived— she never doubted it. This love which He had given to others, had filled her soul with such a love as she had never known. She, who had loved so many, seemed to gather every love into one great adoring passion, which blazed around Him like the colors of the sun-rise around the world. With eyes alight with faith, she passed through the Garden of Gethesemane. She stood with Mary by the cross, holding the power through the darkness—until, with His own lips He had declared it finished.

But was it finished? Only the old condition. He had said 'I shall arise again." She held aloft His promise. The tears were raining down her cheeks. The darkness of the tomb might hide His glory, as the clouds for a few minutes hid the sun—but only would it shine the brighter when the mist was swept away.

And Mary—whom much He had forgiven—Mary at whom Simon had pointed the finger of scorn. Mary—the Magdalene—the former sinner, was the first to give the news of His resurrection to the world.

She seemed to hear the shouts of victory. She stopped. The island was a blaze of glory—earth—sea—sky, and trees and flowers, drifted into one great ball of brilliant light, out of which stepped the form of love and beauty, with hand reached out in blessing for the world. He lived! Her brother could be healed. She never doubted it; she only had to call the power.

*　*　*

She slept out in the star-light and awoke with the first dawn. What a night it had been—what an awakening! A new incarnation. The old self with its continual cry for human love was lifted up on shining wings—into the vastness of a love in which all others faded like the light of suns and stars in the great blaze of Heaven's glory.

No heart aches now. No torn emotions. No separation from the loved ones. No fear that love would pass away. One wish alone she had—to live with such a love as this —to live and serve.

*　*　*

With the light of triumph shining in her eyes—eager as Mary Magdalene to give the news of the resurrection— she ran down the mountain. Never had her bare feet gone so swiftly over the heavy stones.

Arthur was almost startled as she rushed towards him. The power that she had gathered on the heights had robed her with a glory visible even to his holden eyes.

"Arthur, He lives," she cried as she held out her hands toward him. "He lives—He lives—so why should you be sick?"

He sought for explanation by throwing the blame upon another.

"It is the will of God," he said.

"No—it is not," she answered, strongly. "The book you gave me did not tell me *that*—and you said that you believed it all. If you believe it all, then how can you be sick?"

He did not want to say another thing to shatter her faith. He was glad when she began to talk about her brother. It was much easier to believe these truths for him.

My brother will be well," she said. "He will be well —dear, dear Akana. I seem to see those hands of love upon his scars. Those hands which touched blind eyes— and made them see. Arthur it is so beautiful. Why did you never tell me this before?"

A sense of shame came over him at his ingratitude and gross neglect. Like a miser with his locked-up gold, he had lived in a land where people starved for want of what he could have given.

"Akana will be well," she said again, "but you must come with me to see him. You must tell him all. You must tell him of this Christ, the healer. You can tell it in such lovely words. You have known Him so much longer than I have."

Had he known Him so much longer? There are some we know when we first meet them. Others we know all our lives—but never know. He had known his Bible— clung to it for his salvation in another world. Known the character of the man Jesus—but never known the Christ this girl had touched.

"And we shall see our Island as I saw it in the dream," she happily continued. "Only ten thousand times better —because we've found the One the fishers left their nets to follow."

Perhaps he caught the vision with her; the vision of a perfect world. Could he refuse to be a link in forming that great chain of love? Could he refuse the leper's call? He could not say those things were meant for a world two thousand years ago. The same world lived today. The lepers still were here. If he were true to his religion, he must stand for it now.

"Lilinoe," he said with an effort, "I will go with you to where your brother is. If it should cost my life, I'll do it. I have lived within the covers of my Bible all my days, but yet have never known it as you do. I have read His promises without the great belief which made me claim them. I had to come into what I thought your heathen darkness before I gained the light. You have asked my help to cleanse the leper—I cannot in His name refuse."

He walked in the opposite direction as he spoke. The rain began to fall, but he didn't hurry to get under cover; he turned his face up to it, and let it fall on him like a baptism from heaven. One of the many rainbows broke in the sky and shone down on him like the smile of God. A sense of sudden happiness, such as he had never known, flooded his whole being.

The girl had followed him, holding the open Bible in her hand. Smiling, she held it out to him—"you can take it now," she said, "I've got it all inside—I seem to have swallowed it into my heart, and it throbs and sings there as a bird in the sun."

"Keep it," he answered gently, "I have so many more."

She sensed he wanted to be alone, and she left him without another word, but with both arms clasped tightly round the book, like the arms of a loving mother, round her new born child.

CHAPTER XIV
THE JOURNEY TO THE CAVE

The night was ideal when they started for the cave. The moon was big and gold. Sea and sky were a warm blaze of light. The atmosphere was kissed by the scent of a thousand flowers. Everything was still as it had been before the break of dawn.

Lilinoe's face was triumphant with a certainty of victory—and Arthur felt himself gain strength by treading in her foosteps, though his courage had almost failed him when he saw the rugged cliffs and dizzy heights they must ascend—and then descend before they reached the cave.

She got the quick impression of his fear and took his hand in hers. "I know the way and you do not," she said, with that sweet love which is the chief note of Hawaiian utterance. "You trust to me—I will not let you fall."

Her assurance was his inspiration. Scaling the rocks in front of him, watching his every footstep—with the golden flowers wreathed on her hair, like a crown of fallen stars, she looked like some wonderful spirit of the moonlight, dropped from the sky to guide a soul to Heaven.

His heart was beating fast. His breath came quickly. One false step on that dizzy height and they would be hurled into the blackness of the great abyss.

She seemed to sense his every fear and was always ready with a soothing word. He got the power of the vibration even if those words were spoken in a language that he could not understand. He kept his eyes upon her like a mariner on a guiding star. He did not dare to look back for a moment—but more than once he felt peculiarly sensitive that someone was behind them—someone who knew the ground as well as his guide—who crept beneath the rocks and rugged stones—lifting his head occasionally to make sure of their track.

They ascended the highest point and looked down on the sea. Bathed in the moonlight the scene was wildly desolate. Legend and history wrote itself on every rock outlined against the landscape. The tide was coming in with the force of a Kamahamaha's army. It seemed as if the voices of the past were shouting through the booming billows as they roared into the hidden caves and beat their power out on the cliffs, throwing their spray aloft like shining fountains, turned by the moon's bright rays to showers of gold. The girl did not suggest that he was tired, or would like to rest. The night was very short—much was to be accomplished before dawn.

They gained the other side of the sand—and climbing over a ridge, entered one of those wild forests of nature where human foot has seldom trodden, and where "many a flower is born to blush unseen."

"This is the only way that we can reach the cave," she whispered. "The passage underground would be too difficult for you. No trail has been cut here and I do not want to cut one—but if you hold my hand you will not lose the way."

She had no need to give him such a warning. He held to her like a man to the mast of a ship in a storm, as they fought their way through the unspoiled tropical jungle where nature had had her own sweet will to freely indulge her unlimited extravagance. Up hill and down hill they went—over rocks and stones—through narrow passages where moss grown heights shut out the light of the moon—and down which waterfalls roared like thunder. Wading through babbling streams, through grasses high as wheat—catching their feet in snares of serpent-like vines—tangles of ferns—and prickly bushes. Like cold slabs of marble the long leaves of the banana trees rubbed against their faces—and ghostly in the weird light the long leaves of the laulima, stretched their many hands overhead. Every turn seemed to bring out some new wonder in this uncut wilderness of beauty. Here and there a wild garden of red and white lilies flashed out amidst a network of tangled grass, mingling their scent with the fragrance of roses—and their brightness with the silvery foliage of the kukui. Onwards—onwards—through the smothering abundance of nature, until gaining a slippery height, the soil gave way beneath their feet and they began to slip downwards, rather than walk.

Arthur had never tobogganed, but he had watched the boys many times in the winter when the ice was thick on the hill near their home. He had often wondered what such a sensation would be like—but he would never need to wonder again. Slipping and sliding they descended the hill—the girl laughing as merrily as the rosy-cheeked children out in the snow.

He was beginning to wish this experience would end, when suddenly their feet touched the ground, and they stood surrounded by fern-draped, flower-grown walls, in one of the grandest conservatories that nature's artistic hand ever laid out. So lonely—so weirdly desolate—yet with it all so beautiful—it might have been built as a secret hiding place for the gods—where unhampered and secure they could work their silent wonders for the universe. The beauty of the scene was shut out from

above by a leafy roof of trees, through the delicate lace-
work of which, the moonlight fell in showers of gold—
dancing across the thick carpet of leaves like little golden
crowned fairies, and glittering in shining beams upon the
deep pool of silvery water—white as the driven snow.

"He is in there," she whispered, pointing to the vine-
twined overhanging rocks which hid the entrance to the
cave. "To reach him we must swim under the ledge."

"Only I cannot swim," he said, "and the water is
cold. Can't he come out to us?"

She shook her head. "The moonlight is too bright,"
she answered. "When it is dark he steals into the forest
and gathers fruit, and goes down to the beach to bathe.
But there is one other way to reach him, and we can take
it—follow me."

It needed all his courage to do so, but she was holding
his hand again in that firm, warm grip—gentle, yet com-
pelling obedience. They climbed a few more rocks and
then paused by one bigger and more mighty than the
others. She stooped low and divided fern and bushwood,
cutting away the vines with her grass hook, until a hidden
hole disclosed the subterranean passage. Bending almost
to earth, she crept in like a rabbit, and instinctively he
followed. The ferns and trees swung back and closed
the entrance. Out of the golden moonlight the blackness
was dense before his eyes. It seemed as if he were buried
in a grave. A fear such as he had never known gripped
his heart, and for a moment he lost confidence in his
guide. How did he know but what this was a trap?

"Have you no light?" he asked, abruptly. "Where
are you taking me? How can I see in this Egyptian
darkness? I did not expect that it would be like this."

"Hush!" she said gently. "I know the way. Hold to
my hand and you cannot fall."

His eyes began to grow accustomed to the darkness. Away down the awful stairway formed of jutting rock, he could see a dim light from the other entrance—and the shining gleam of moonlit water. It was almost more ghostly than the darkness—yet it brought with it a gleam of hope—that out of this living grave, there was a way.

"Don't be afraid," she said again. "This is the only means by which we can reach him, if you cannot swim."

"It's terribly dangerous," he answered. "One slip—"

Her laugh rang through the rocks and hollows, awakening echoes hitherto unknown.

"Only, you could not slip, when I have hold of you," she said.

Her words brought in a flash a scene long ago forgotten, which came with a new light to him now. In memory he was carried from the darkness of his surroundings to one of those sudden snowstorms in Wisconsin. Through the whirling flakes and blinding wind, the milkman had come to their door to deliver the milk. His little boy sat in the cart, muffled to the ears against the storm. He remembered how his Aunt, with her usual benevolence, knowing the rough road they had to travel, had asked the child:

"Would you like to stay with us until the morning? Are you not afraid of the storm and the dark?"

Looking through the window he saw the smile on the child's face as he answered: "No—not afraid—father knows the way."

The memory of this somehow gave him strength. The faith of the little child entered his soul with a beautiful sense of security and peace. Unconsciously he found himself repeating: "The darkness and the light are both alike to Thee."

The path began to grow a little easier. The over-hanging rocks were not so close. Once able to lift his head and stand erect, he felt the power. He rejoiced in this victory over fear—small though it might have seemed to many, yet great to his undeveloped soul.

The jutting rocks had almost cut his shoes to pieces. His clothes were torn and his hands scratched—but he had scarcely noticed it in his great desire to get out of this living grave.

They reached the end sooner than he had hoped—climbed the rocks above the water, and passing through a flower-grown arch, entered the cave. The room was long and winding—stretching far back into the moun-tain. Ferns in abundance grew out of the walls and ceiling. The heavy leadges were moss-grown and green. On one of these ledges which jutted out from the wall and formed a lofty throne—a man was sitting. He had lighted a torch of dry lahala and the weird glow shone red across the floor and ceiling—and blazed on his handsome young face and powerful limbs. He looked like a mighty god of strength and power—born to hold the throne of the Island instead of the stony seat of a hidden cave.

The girl rushed up to him and throwing her arms about his neck, she kissed him on the lips and eyes.

"Akana," she cried, gladly. "You are going to be well. It is wonderful—so wonderful; too wonderful for me to tell you—so I had to bring the one who knows the story—here."

CHAPTER XV

THE LEPER

Arthur sat down upon the stones. Hurt and bruised, with his limbs aching from the long walk, he felt it was he who needed the physician not this strong young monarch on the throne.

"To make me well," the bitter voice spoke through the darkness. "To make me well. Who is there could do that? If the gods could have granted me deliverance, surely they would have done it long ago."

He broke off with a sob which echoed through the cave. There was something so heart-rending in it that it stirred the listener to the soul, in a desire to help this powerful young man to escape from the dreadful disease.

"But Akana, it's true," the girl said, nothing daunted. "There is so much to tell you—but he'll tell it all. Let him sit here, and talk, while I gather the fruits for you upon the mountain."

"Did you bring the flowers of the heights, and the wanaao?" he asked, like one who had not noticed what she said.

"You don't need them any more," she answered. "You will not want them when you hear what he has to tell."

She kissed him again and slipped out of the cave—making a dive into the shining waters. They could hear her softly singing as she swam to shore.

"The first time she has sung for months," the young man said. "She used to have a voice like a bird. We always sang together on the mountains, before I went away, and all this came."

The light of the torch went out while he was speaking, and he stretched his strong young arms in the darkness.

"Come out of here," he said. "I want you to see the moon and stars—I am tired of this bondage—and it is no place for you."

Arthur had no desire to move, knowing the only exit could be made through the dark passage or else by water that he could not swim.

"I thought you were in hiding," he said, gently. "Hadn't you better stay just where you are?"

"I know—but sometimes I get reckless," he replied. "But for my sister it would not matter if they found me. Aren't you afraid of the disease?"

The terror of the trip had wiped out every thought of it. "I believe it can be healed," he answered, remembering the mission which had brought him there.

The man laughed harshly in the darkness. "Yes— so she thinks, dear girl," he said. "She gets the healing flowers from the mountains. She prays to all her gods to help me. She comes here every day and holds the secret of my whereabouts. O, but for her —I'd quit the game and let them take me. What did she bring you here for?" He asked the question suddenly.

"She thought that I could help you," Arthur answered.

"How?"

He was so long in finding a reply that the Hawaiian thought he had not heard and asked again: "How can you help me? What do you know? Maybe you are just a spy sent from the coast—and have made her the goat to find my whereabouts."

"No," answered Arthur with conviction. "Believe me—I'm no spy—I want to help you, but it's hard to make you understand."

"Why?"

"Because I am not sure myself."

"Then don't tell things you are not sure of, that would do no good. You're from the coast, Maybe you have traveled far. Tell me of things in other lands. I've always wanted to travel, I'd planned to go to other countries— I'd got it all arranged when all this came."

"How did you find it out?"

"They found it out for me. I left our little home seven years ago. Somehow I wanted different things from what we had. The men came from the city. They told me of the things that are over there. Girls came with different colored eyes and hair, from those who live amongst us. I always thought my sister had the prettiest face in all the world—but then you know she was my sister. I liked eyes like the sky at noonday, and hair like the gold you see in the sunrise. I went to Waikiki and found them. But pretty eyes and faces hide a heart that's often shallow. I got work quickly and made money— spent it all—had lots of fun. "No boy could ride a surf-board like I rode it—even if I say it myself. The blue-eyed girls were all in love with me. I spent my time teaching them surf-board, making leis for them, and teaching them to ride. They went back to the coast— and wrote me letters. "Of course their parents never knew. Folks from the coast can do most what they like at Waikiki—but when they get back to their homes it's different. The boys grew jealous of me. Maybe I was too popular—I don't know. They had it in for me in lots of ways. It seems I'd taken one fellow's girl. I told him he could have the rest of them, but I wanted that girl—

with eyes like a sunny morning. She liked me, too—liked me far better than she liked him—but he was from the coast, he had no colored blood." He stopped a moment. "God," he said, bitterly, "how I prayed for a white face. She told me that she loved me—but she could not marry me—because she wanted a child—she could not nurse a colored baby—and I told her that was not love. I did not blame her for not wanting a Hawaiian. None of them do when it comes down to marriage. They'll take all that you'll give them in the way of pleasure, but when it comes to mixing of blood, it is different.

"The other boy who wanted her got jealous. He was tall and blonde, like she was, always dressed well, and had pink fingernails. I had not his manners nor elegant appearance, but I had the strength of the Hawaiian, and he knew it. "He and the other fellows had it in for me. I did not want to fight. I knew I could lick the whole bunch with a single hand,they were only like a lot of puppets in a show, to me. But of course the fight had to come and it came just when I did not want it. I was on the beach with her. You know the beach at Waikiki— when the moon is big and full and the waves come washing over the sand—when there's music and song, and everyone is happy. It was a shame to fight, but I had to do it. I licked them all and she was proud of me. She was nearer to me then than she had ever been. I remember how she put her little hand in mine. (She had such tiny hands—just like a doll's. I was so big and strong beside her.) And she said: 'Akana, I would rather be a man with colored blood, and brave and strong like you, than I would be those young dandies—who had to run away.' It made me happy, I can tell you. The victory of the fight was nothing—I hadn't shown my strength one-quarter. I had enough to face an army. I did not call that fighting, and I told her so. It was only like one might have whipped some troublesome dogs that had been barking after you. But they were not through with me, and I knew it. The next day came—the next, and next. The girl did not come to meet me by the water. I saw her once upon the beach, and she nodded coolly to me—and went on her way. Bit by bit they got it noised abroad I was a leper. I did not believe it—I had always been so well. I'd never had a sickness, but they forced me to believe that it was so. It came to me like a bolt out of a clear sky.

"They came in a great body to arrest me. They knew my strength, for they had seen me in the fight. They took me to some specialist, who claimed that it was true. They were going to send me over to the Island. They shut me in quarantine until the time, but I fooled them, as you see. I got away. They have never known yet how I did it. We natives have a knowledge of the land that fools the white man every time. I came back to the ground where I was born—I came back to the sister that I had neglected. It seems like prison in this cave—but yet it's my own land—and it is home."

Arthur was helpless as to what to say. A prayer such as he had never prayed rose to his lips.

"I have a book that I could lend you," he suggested.

The young man answered something like his sister.

"I never want to read. I like real things—the things that live—not things that men make up. Besides, I could not see in here. I climb upon the overhanging rocks each morning and look into the pool. The water is so clear— so luminous, and bright. I watch the pictures in it—not reflections—pictures of other lands that come and go. I travel there, and I forget my sickness—I see myself just as I ought to be—just as I was before they branded me a leper——"

"Just as you will be," Arthur found himself saying. The voice that spoke was his own—and yet it did not seem his own—but the conviction struck right home.

"Did you say that?" the young man asked.

"Yes," answered Arthur, slowly.

"It sounded like the voices that I hear sometimes. This place is full of spooks—and voices. Gee—If we only had a light!"

"I believe you will be well," he said again. "There is One who can make you so."

"And where is He?"

Arthur cleared his throat.

"Did you never hear of Christ?" he asked.

"O, many a time!" The note of disappointment in the voice was deep. "They used to talk about Him in the churches when they got up and told us how to die. I went to church sometimes in Honolulu. I liked the music—not the talk. I guess you're one of those good people—maybe that's why you've come to me."

"No," answered Arthur, "if I were, I'd make it plainer to you."

He paused a moment. The dampness of the cave brought on a fit of coughing.

"You don't seem extra well, yourself," Akana said. "It's bad to have a cough like that."

"I haven't been well," Arthur answered, "but I'm getting better now." Again he did not seem to voice the words. Someone seemed to be speaking through his lips. "I think He's healing me."

"Who's healing you? This fellow you call Christ?"

"Yes," Arthur said, with positive conviction. "I know that He can make me well."

"Tell me about Him. I went once to a picture show in Honolulu, and they put His picture on the screen. Nice looking guy—but not like us. He wore clothes like a woman."

Considering the consciousness he had to deal with, Arthur tried not to appear shocked.

"Where is He now?" Akana asked.

"He ascended into Heaven, and sitteth at the right hand of God the Father," Arthur answered, repeating word by word the church service he had known from boyhood up.

"Into Heaven? That's not much good to me, and as for God you call the Father, I've got no use for Him. He's made a pretty bungle of my life."

"O, hush!" said Arthur, really pained at such expression. "You must not talk like that."

"Why not? They told me that there was one God —those fellows who stand before that big book which I could not read in a whole lifetime—and those that fight with drums and tambourines at the street corners. I listened to them, and they wanted to—what do you call it—? To convert me. I did not follow all they said. I tell you that I have no use for any God that puts a fellow into flames, because he wants to live his life the way he wants to. I've not been a bad fellow on the whole. I know I've made some slips—but if I thought a God away in Heaven had sent this suffering to me, because I hadn't done just what He ordered—I tell you, I would fight it. That's not the kind of God I want—and I don't believe that any God who made this lovely world for us to live and love in—I don't believe that such a God would wish that anyone should suffer. I've got my picture of a God—but not, I guess, the one you have. My God is like my father. I was full of mischief when I was a kid.

What boy with pep in him is not? There was no harm in me—my father knew it, though he gave me many a licking—never to hurt, but just to make me mind.

"Maybe my sister told you how we lived in the grass hut up on the mountain. We hadn't much in that grass hut—only a few things that my father made, like chairs and tables cut out of the trees—and a few treasures that my mother saved of ancestors long past. One day my father brought a box of matches home. We had never seen matches. We hadn't any use for lights—we went to bed when darkness fell, and got up with the dawn. I remember how my father struck one of those matches— and how we laughed to see the cunning little blaze. Then how he put them in a box—and told us not to touch them. I was a lad full of mischief, and when his back was turned, I went straight for the box. I didn't know the danger of the blaze until the grass of our small hut caught fire and the roof was burning overhead. I tried to put it out, but it had spread too quickly—and frightened at the deed I'd done, I rushed into the woods to hide. My mother and my sister were gathering berries down the mountain. My father saw the blaze in the distance and came rushing back, hoping to save the home. He and my mother fought the flames—but they had got too big a hold—the hut burnt down and all that we had in it.

"Then I remember how they called for me. They knew I must have had the matches. I remember how my father threatened what he was going to do, when he laid hands on me. I got more scared, and went further into the woods until my arms and feet got scratched with the bushes, and I fell in the tangles of the vine. I didn't want to go back home. I knew the home had gone—and I could see nothing but the punishment awaiting me. I felt like a little outcast in that lonely place—and I longed to get back to my father—if only I could believe he would forgive me for all the mischief I had done. I lay down on the leaves and cried my heart out—sobbing and sobbing till I fell asleep.

"I was awakened in the early morning by great strong arms lifting me gently. They were my father's arms. I thought the rain was falling on my face—but it was my father's tears. He and my mother had sought and called for me all night—but failed to find me—and by the morning they were sure that I was burnt up in the hut.

"He carried me gently not to wake me—and then he laid me in my mother's arms. I had been a bad boy, but he forgot it—he forgot everything in the great joy of finding me. Then how they bathed my little scratched body —and how my mother kissed by little blistered feet —and took off her only wrap to cover me—because I shivered and seemed cold. My little sister ran into the woods to bring me fruit—and put a lei of flowers around my neck. We had no home, for I had burnt it—but my father set to work to build it up again—and we slept out underneath the trees, and no one ever said a word to me about it.

"O, that's the kind of God I'd like to find. We've all burnt huts down in our lives—and everyone of us have played with fire—we've all been bad and disobedient —but I'm looking for a God who understands. Seems like our mistakes to Him must be like mine were to my father. I want a God who's older than we are—and knows we haven't wisdom. My father had the eyes to see I did not mean what I had done. Why, if we'd got the light— there isn't one of us would sin. We're just a lot of little children—and most of us don't know any better.

"If I had known, to play with fire would burn my father's house down—make him lose all he had—

although it wasn't much—and make my mother cry—
would I have done it? No—of course I wouldn't. We
sin because we've only got a glimpse of light. We don't
see in the way our parents see—and it seems to me, in
the eyes of the big God, we're just such little children
as we are in our father's eyes. So if this God you speak
of is like what you say, He couldn't have it in for me,
because I wasn't all I ought to be.

It was a new life I met in the city—and I played with
it like moths do with a light. They don't know that
sometime they will singe their wings. The disobedient
boy that goes out on the surf-board deserves to bump his
nose—but you can't say he deserves to drown. I want
a God who takes you in His arms just like my father did.
I want a God who cares."

"He does care," answered Arthur, "not a sparrow
falls to the ground without He cares."

Akana had picked up many a fallen bird and healed
its broken wing. The words appealed to him—but still
he was not satisfied.

"Then if He cares," he said, "He surely cannot want
to keep me here. Here in this hiding place away from all.
He cannot wish to see me sick."

"He sent His Christ to heal the sick."

"Are you quite sure He did?"

"Yes—I believe it."

"And does this Christ still live?"

A sob rose in the leper's throat.

"He is alive forever, I believe."

"You say He is the son of your God?"

"Yes."

The young man seemed to be thinking. Perhaps he
caught the dawn of glory at that moment.

"The son of God—my, what a son He must have been —son of the God that you tell of. Was there anything impossible for Him to do?"

"Nothing."

Again they were silent. Like his sister, the young man was contemplating the vastness of the power.

"Our gods, the gods that we believe in, live in differ- ent things—in water, flowers, the moon, the stars, but this one God you tell of, holds our world. You say this Christ man was sent by Him, to make sick people well?"

"Sent to redeem the world," said Arthur, struggling for words to make things plain.

"And He had all the power to do it? The Kahunas used to call that power; they called on every god to send it to them, and then they flung it out into the air and people died because they willed it so, because the gods were angry. Did this Christ you tell of, call power like that?"

"God was His Father. He called His Father's name and His Father sent the power to Him. Sometimes it came like a mighty rushing wind; it brought life to the dead; it swept over the diseased bodies of the lepers and they were cleansed; it poured into the hearts of men and made them long to serve Him; it gave strength to crip- pled limbs; sight to blind eyes—there was nothing im- possible for it to do."

"My—what a power it must have been. I never knew a power like that, but I always knew there was one. If such a power could come into this cave, it must break down the walls and make me free. If I could see this Christ you speak of—where does He live, where can I find Him?"

"His power is everywhere," Arthur replied. "People believed in it, so they were made well. One woman said in the midst of a great crowd 'if I can touch His garment I shall be well.' "

"And did she touch it?"

"Yes—and she was made well."

"Where is this Christ?" he asked again. "I want to find Him. I know if He is what you say, He will heal me as He healed the others. Where can I find Him? Is He on this Island?"

"He is here and everywhere."

"But you said He was ascended into the heavens?"

"That makes no difference. He is ever ready, answering those who call."

"Then, if I call Him, He will come?"

"Yes, I believe it."

Their conversation was stopped by the soft singing of the girl in the distance. She was swimming through the luminous water, holding with one hand above her head, a bunch of wild bananas, and a leaf of thimble berries she had gathered.

She slipped her dress on quickly over her bathing suit, shook the wet drops from her abundant hair, and joined them in the cave. Her face was triumphant.

She had no fear for her brother now, no question for his safety. She had accepted the promise for his healing. She knew she did not leave him alone, for the Christ in which she believed, was there to lighten his darkness, and to set him free.

CHAPTER XVI

RESURRECTION

A storm was coming, one of the quick storms of the Island. Lilinoe had sensed it in the air. The moon had gone in, they were walking in darkness. Her arm was around Arthur, as the arm of a mother around her child. The rain began to beat upon their faces, the wind to blow.

"It will soon be over," she said gently. "There is a cave above the sea where we can shelter."

She had no fear of the descending storm; she had faced such things a thousand times, and there was something so beautiful in this newly found happiness, that she wanted to sit still with him, and talk about it. They went into the shelter of the cave; the waves were beating hard upon the rocks beneath, the tide was rising. The same old nervous fear gripped Arthur's heart. They could not see how high the waters were but he could feel the spray upon his face. If the cave were to be flooded, he could not swim as she did, besides, one of those giant waves could sweep them in a moment out to sea.

"Are you afraid?" she asked, sensing his fear.

"A little," he confessed, "are you?"

"Afraid? how could I be? To a worse storm than this, He just said 'Peace' and all was still. Arthur, you said He still lives. If He still lives, and He is with us, then cannot He say Peace now, just as He said it then?"

She was showing him his lack of faith, of practical belief in the promises he had read so many times. He felt like a sinner in the presence of a reproving angel. Still the waves were mounting, the cave was flooded now. He left her side, and feeling along the wall, climbed to a higher ridge for safety. She did not seem to notice, her hands were clasped upon her lap; She was looking up-wards, the clouds had suddenly parted, and once more the moon's soft primrose light was shining on the sea.

"And immediately there was a great calm," he heard her say, and the words brought rebuke to his doubting, fearing soul.

* * *

After they had left him, Akana continued to sit on the rock, wrapped in thought. A light had come to him. —a sudden hope. His simple child-like mind, unsatiated by a babel of conflicting creeds, grasped the simplicity of the truth that Arthur had expressed. There was no veil of doubt between him and the wonders that the power of this one God could do. He thought of boisterous seas where rested all the islands of the world. He thought of nations far and wide, like insects gathered on those islands. He thought of trees that grew and birds that sang, and animals and reptiles, even insects in the sand, and he thought of the vast love which had created all.

His strength seemed born anew, courage returned, and the question arose within his heart—why was he hiding here, why for the first time in his life had he not dared to face the situation? If he had the disease they claimed he had, why had he tried to run away from his pursuers? He had never known what it was to be a coward, he was prepared to face all now; he would go into the daylight, for he knew he was not alone. If this Christ still lived, and he believed He did, because this messenger from God had told him so, then he did not

need to wait for Him to come in person, he would go
forth to meet Him.

A rest, such as he had never known since he entered
the cave, fell over him. All fear and all belief in sickness,
left him. He slipped down quietly upon the floor, and
with his face buried in his arms, he fell asleep.

* * *

It was not the moon's rays that awoke him. The light
that had transformed the cave, was brighter than the
sunrise. Moon, sun, and stars seemed melted into one.

Whose were the arms that lifted him so strongly?
Whose were the tears of love and pity falling on his face?
Who stood beside him, bringing light into his darkness?
Who was it wept with him, who cared because he suffered? He did not seek to know. The beauty of that all-
enfolding love was far too great for question. He rested
in its healing strength, as when a little child, he rested
on his father's heart.

The hands that touched his were the hands of the
One who cleansed the lepers. The power that swept
across his body, was the power of Him who raised the
dead, the One with whom all things were possible. His
soul went out to that compassionate soul, with the confidence of one who recognized a love that was stronger
than a brother's. He saw all false beliefs shrivel like
tindered leaves, all dark illusions fade as the ugly dreams
fade with the awakening light of morning. Through the
power of that great healing love, he saw himself a perfect
man. The power in which he now believed—the power
which broke the seals of the imprisoning tomb, had set
him free.

* * *

Arthur returned to his cottage, but not to rest. He was amazed that he was not weary. He sat by the open window in the fast waning starlight. His mind was too active for sleep. A great responsibility had been thrown upon him. He had been called to prove the statements of the religion he professed. He had always been sincere in his belief. He had attended his home church when he was able, and with a painfuly sick body, had sat opposite the beautiful stained glass window, with his eyes fixed on the picture of the healing of the sick. Looking on this, he had confessed with the congregation to his belief in God the Father Almighty—but had he ever stopped to think what that Almighty meant.

He reviewed his narrow cramped life; saw it as it might have been, saw it as it was. He was only twenty-five, but he felt as if he had wasted a life time; wasted it in thoughts of sickness; hugged his beliefs in God to his heart, when he ought to have been sharing the grand message with the world. Possibly it was the inheritance of the thoughts of an ancestry of missionaries from which he came, that stirred an unawakened fire in his soul, and longing to go forth to heal and teach in the name of the Christ in which he had always believed, to teach with the new understanding he had gained, gained through this seemingly heathen girl, who, in the twinkling of an eye had grasped the truths he had never until now understood. He saw himself the prodigal, strayed far from His Father's house, sitting among the husks of sickness, lonely —forsaken, and then, through the darkness, there shot forth the star of hope, the memory that though he had left his father, that Father had never left him, and that he had only to return, and the welcome awaited him, the welcome to the love that he had always had but never appreciated.

"I will arise and go unto my Father," he repeated these words aloud. There was no question in the prodigal's heart, as to whether his Father would receive him, for when he was yet a great way off, his Father saw him—and he was so far away, but the moment he set forth with longing, eternal love came forth to meet him—the past wiped out with the confession of his sin.

A penitent he knelt before the open window, and bowing his head upon his hands, he poured forth his whole soul in prayer.

"O, Christ divine, and infinitely tender, a penitent I come to Thee, knowing so little of Thy great love, and never even stretching forth my hand to touch the healing of Thy garment; my consciousness of sickness stronger than my consciousness of Thee, I want to drop the weight of wasted years behind me, and as the blind man by the roadside, cried for sight, I pray for eyes to see the beauty of a love, which will make we whole. With new enlighenment, I pray for courage to go forth to prove to all I meet, that the healing power still lives, that the love of God is changeless, that the Christ is still the same—yesterday, today and forever.

"Give me of Thy great love which conquers all things; Thy strength to tread the path. Give me of Thy divine compassion which burns out self in love of service. And if it should be that I am wanted here—grant me my healing, that by my life and light I may show other souls the way to Thee. Amen."

He lifted his head with a sense of peace and joy stealing into his heart like the voice of God in silent answer. The first call of the dawn came through the evaporating darkness. It showed the faces of the pink hibiscus peeping through the window. He walked to the door and drew in long breaths of the reviving air. Nature was rubbing her sleepy eyes in response to the awakening voices. A sky lark suddenly soared upwards, bursting into a rapturous song of praise. His soul seemed lifted with it. Unconsciously he reached out his arms to embrace the whole world.

And in this great universe God needed every unit that He had created. The joy of it came to him with a mighty thrill—

God needed him.

Chapter XVII

AKANA TELLS OF HIS HEALING

Down by the beach, Lilinoe watched the dawn. She was not praying—she had asked—she knew the answer now was given. Her eyes were full of that sweet love which must have been in the eyes of the One who said: "Father, I think Thee—Thou hast heard Me."

Her expression did not change from its calm serenity when Ewaliko came rushing towards her. His eyes were wild with terror. He caught her hands in his, and pointed to the distance.

"They are coming," he cried. "They are coming—the men from over the sea. The men with uniforms and bright buttons—and stars. They are coming to take Akana—I know it. I saw them in my dreams. Let us go quickly and get him out of the cave."

She smiled gently in response and drew him down by her side. Her quietness calmed him.

'Nothing can harm Akana," she answered. "If these men came, what would it matter? Akana is safe. He is enfolded in such a love as he has never known. A love I have found. A love which will always be there to take care of him."

He looked at her in perplexity, and then said, sadly:

"He came, then—the one I said was coming to claim you."

"Yes, Ewaliko, he came," she replied, "and I am going with him, it matters not where."

He forgot the errand on which he had come. He picked up his fallen instrument and walked slowly away —his head drooping low—like the head of a flower struck by the sharpness of an icy wind.

She did not detain him—did not move from where she was sitting. The men who had just arrived by the boat came towards her. They were followed by a crowd of natives, attracted by their uniforms and the strangeness of their errand.

"They are seeking your brother Akana," cried one of the boys. "They say he is hidden here on the Island."

She arose and went forward to meet them. For a moment they stood without speaking—almost dumb-founded by her unusual beauty. It was not the sensuous attraction of the great, wonderful eyes, the dusky skin, and the flowing black hair garlanded with the wreath of scarlet flowers—but it was the great illumination which they could not understand, the power of the Spiritual forces which she still held.

"You want my brother?" she asked. "He is here. I will bring him to you."

The natives who had declared that Akana had gone years ago, and never returned, threw up their hands and gazed at her in amazement. She was walking away, but she suddenly stopped and looked with a smile across the blue waters. The sight she saw was very familiar, but it was a sight she had missed for so many sad years. The sight of a man rising out of the waters, mounting his surf-board and steering his course over the waves with the same natural ease that a clever machinist would steer his car over mountain and dale. Strong—grand and beau-tiful, he stepped on the shore—his brown skin sparkling with water—his face glowing with healthy exercise. He reached his powerful arms out to his people—and a great cry of joy went up from all.

"It is Akana. Akana come back to us from over the sea."

The men from the coast were losing patience at this long delay.

"Bring us the leper," they cried. "Where have you him hidden?"

Akana laughed in their faces, and held out his hands.

"I am the man you want," he replied. "If I have leprosy, take me to the Island—shut me up there—but wherever I am you cannot put bondage upon me. I am ready to go with you anywhere."

The men looked baffled.

"You are not the one we seek," they cried. "We seek the leper. By wireless we have received information that his sister has hidden him here."

Lilinoe was standing beside him. The likeness between them was too strong to deny the relationship.

"It is Akana," the natives declared. "The boy who left us for the city long, long ago, and we waited and wept and longed for his return. We knew his father and mother—and he is no leper."

The young man smiled at his sister.

"I will go back with them to prove I am the one they are seeking," he said. "I will tell them the wonderful story that all may be cleansed."

He strolled away by the side of the officers, talking interestingly to them, pointing out the historic spots on the Island where he had been raised—entering bit by bit into the details of his life.

"No wonder you were in hiding," said one of the men. "Such a jealous accusation—*you* a leper, indeed. A man without a blemish upon him, strong as a lion—with the healthiest of skin."

"I was a leper," he replied, "but now I am cleansed." The officers smiled.

"Men don't get cleansed so easily, I fear," he said. "A great wrong has been done you."

"It was no wrong—it was a blessing in disguise," Akana answered.

"A blessing in disguise—to have some jealous fellow brand you with a curse like leprosy!" cried the officer. "Why, man, if you were not so sensible to look at, I'd think you were a little off your head."

"If you knew all, you would not think so," said Akana. "If you knew how I cursed my fate in the beginning and cried to every god for help, and for deliverance. Branded as a leper! Driven into a cave to die; I, who had been free as the winds and waves and morning sunshine! My sister helped me all she could—bringing the healing herbs and flowers by night. She gathered me fruit and brought the freshest water from the spring. She tried the healing of our fathers—but I did not seem to get the help. Yet I believed in all those healings—I had seen results so many times. Above all things, I knew this world was full of power. A power the old Kahunas understood—a power which, when gathered and sent out like a rushing wind, was able to destroy or to uplift. I had watched it in the storms—in the force of the waves—and in the destructive hurricane—and I had thought so many times, if we could tap that power, there would be nothing impossible for us to do. Well, the man from the coast came to the cave, and told me how this power, rightly used, could heal the sick, and even raise the dead. I saw just how it could be possible, for I have felt it bubbling through me like new life when I was riding on my surf-board. It struck me then, that if our bodies made connection with it—it would be like the new sap rushing through a tree—reviving us from day to day, filing us with that vital energy which knows no death—which makes life everlasting.

"He told me all this power belonged to one great God—a God of Love—who gave it for our use, and he told me of the man who came to show us all the great things that it could do. And that was how I got my healing. I called the power of that great God. I called the God of Love, and it seemed as if He lifted me on wings of wind, and the sickness of my body dropped away as tindered leaves from the bark of a tree."

The officers stood looking at him. He talked so rapidly; his face was glowing and his eyes inspired. They were carried away by the wonder of his words.

"You are a marvelous specimen of a cleansed leper," said one man at last. "If all could get their healing as rapidly as that, we should not need a leper's isle."

"They could get it just as rapidly," he answered. "If they once touched the power I touched, they could not be unclean."

The men smiled at each other. The beautiful simplicity of these Islanders, they thought. The eldest of them patted Akana on the shoulder.

"Only a leper by belief," he said.

"Yes, by belief," Akana answered, but they failed to grasp the great truth of his words.

Chapter XVIII

INTO ALL THE WORLD

When the calm and beautiful evening had come, Arthur found Lilinoe seated on her favorite rock beside the sea. The sun was setting, and across the golden carpet of the Heavens, fragments of broken, purple clouds were scattered like bunches of fragrant violets thrown by angels' hands.

Arthur had been thinking out the problem of his life. He realized as he had never done, that he had a future —a future which must be dedicated to service.

The command had been, "Go forth to all the world." The promise was, "And I will give you power."

Could he set forth on this alone? Go like the "silent seventy," dependent not even on scrip nor purse? The world looked very cold and very big. He gazed across the island he had learnt to love. It was so warm, so full of heart—a little patch of Heaven here. Could he leave this for lands he did not know? Out of the golden sunset looked—the face of Lilinoe, sweet, lovable and tender.

He thought of all that she had been to him. He went back to the night when they first met, and saw her guiding him across the rocks towards his home. Prophetic picture of the future! Had not her strong hands guided him right to the center of his healing, leading him through the darkness of his sickness to the Christ which made him whole?

163

What mattered nationality? She was woven into his life with a golden thread that no hands could unravel.

She had never been a stranger to him. It seemed as if from all time he had known her; that in the narrow book of his life, pages which had been sealed and missed, were opening. On every page he saw her name and picture. Had he, he often wondered, met her in dreams before they met on this Island on which he seemed to have been washed by waves of circumstance? Vague memories had made him miserable on the night of the luan; they had often made him draw from her in fear, but now they filled his heart with rapture, with a hope that what he had believed a dream, might be a reality.

He had never had a friend in a woman. He had never known what it meant to love. He saw the starved lonely years behind him. He saw the great possibilities in front. He felt like a man who had come out of the desert, and found green fields and cooling waters. There was so much he could do with his life. Could he but keep the faith which had awakened in his soul. Once more his mind turned to the one who had led him to the greater understanding, a heathen girl, he had believed her to be, he looked on her now as his guardian angel, a missionary sent to him to light the way to God. A longing that they might be together for the rest of life overcame him, a knowledge that they both moved in the same vibration, and both loved the same God, swept thoughts of nationality aside. Their souls belonged to each other, and he tried to tell her so, when she joined him in the silence of the place where they first met. This love making was very strange to him, but it was so sincere. She listened, looking far out to sea, then suddenly she drew nearer to him, put her arm round him and laid her cheek against his own. He would have been satisfied for everything to end with the joy of that moment, to have gone out of life with the beautiful memory of what might never be again. The wonder of it was so high that neither spoke. His arms which had always been so helpless where woman was concerned, were slowly responding to the great warmth of her love, and almost before he knew it, he had clasped them around her and drawn her to his heart.

"I love you, Lilinoe," he said, and then again, "I love you. We are of a different nationality I know, but love wipes out all thought of that. I owe everything to you, Lilinoe, yes, everything, even the love I feel towards God. I understand the meaning now of being born again. I want to tell all the world of this new birth I have found, of a redeemer who saves from sin, sickness and death. Will you not go forth with me, Lilinoe, that we may tell the story together?"

Her tears were falling as she laid her hand on his.

"I cry for joy," she said. "It is so beautiful to think you love me—for nothing that we love can ever leave us. That was the teaching of the old Kahuna. I used to dread the time when you would go away. I need not dread it any more—for if you love me, we can never part."

"I have not much in a financial way," he continued. "I've paid my money out in doctors' bills—but I have still a little income—enough for us to travel in His service. Shall we set forth together—Lilinoe—you and I?"

She looked at him with happy eyes and smiling lips.

"And you would take me with you, Arthur?" she said, gently. "Then you must love me very much, for I am not of your people. I have not your fair skin. I do not know your pretty ways. I cannot talk as you do— I can only love."

"But that is all we need," he said. "If we can love, we have solved every problem. If we can love the world, then we can save it. My fault has been that I have never loved. I thought I loved my God—but if I love my God I must love all things—must see in all, that spark of light which is a part of Him. Must see the beautiful in every atom of His divine creation. That means love to God, Lilinoe. You know that love, and I am learning it from you."

"But if I had you with me always," she replied, "I might forget to work for Him. The human love is very sweet. You know the nature of our people—just live and love from day to day. It would be very easy for us both to live in that sweet sunshine—to live up on the mountain with the sky and flowers—but there are other souls that want what we can give, and we must go to tell them of that love which cannot see them sick nor sad. The love which healed my brother; The love which made you well; The love which will take care of me when you have gone away."

"But we could do all this together, Lilinoe," he said. "I have no one in the world but you. Why should I care for race and color?"

"No one but Lilinoe?" she asked. "But what about the One whose love has made you well?"

"I know," he answered, gently. "We are so human, though."

"But if you reach to Him, I will be there," she said. "Wherever He is, I shall be. My work is for the Islands. I do not know your people. My mother was not happy in your land—and if you took me there, and they did not receive me—it would only hurt you many times."

"My people!" he responded. "Where are they, Lilinoe? God knows I have no people. Surely the words, 'my people,' implies those who are nearest to our hearts. I have some scattered relatives, but their interest does not lie with me—and as for what the world calls *friends,* I never found them anywhere outside my pocketbook.

"Then they need you very much," she answered. "Maybe they need the love you did not give them. If you go back to love your land—to love your people—then of course they will love you—and if they love you—you can help them.

"Arthur, I want to go with you, I want to go, only, you know what it would mean, but if you go with Him, you cannot be alone, and I shall be always with you, for do we not love the same dear God, and when I pray then you will kneel beside me and our prayers will go together up to Him. We'll clasp each other's hands then, just as we clasp them now. The birds and flowers, the earth and air, yes, and the big waves of the sea, will all carry my love to you, and we will not be parted."

He looked at her in sheer amazement. She was willing to let him go, and yet he knew she loved him, that the whole of her strong ardent being was yearning for him, and the earth love now in him awakened, was calling to her, even as she called to him. He would have given into his desire and made every excuse for himself, that they must spend their lives together, that she needed him as much as he needed her, but she had seen a wider vision for them both, had seen the life of service, not of self. Again, she was teaching him when he had believed he was the one who was teaching her.

Could he go forth without her? Through the stillness the voice came like a strong command: "Leave all that thou hast—and follow Me."

He lifted his eyes to the sky now bright with stars scattered like golden shells in a sea of blue. The world was very big and mighty, but yet those same stars smiled on every country. The same God watching over all.

"All that thou hast," he found himself repeating. It seemed a hard command—but it gave the wings of freedom to the soul, in place of nets of bondage.

* * *

When Yee Kui brought in the supper tray that night, he paused and looked at Arthur. Between these two there was a beautiful understanding—although they talked little.

"The master has found what he came here for?" he asked.

"Yes, Yee Kui," Arthur responded. "I have found it. I came here sick and miserable. I came here seeking health alone—and getting more and more sick in the search. I was sick because I did not know God. I was seeking His gifts, but closing my eyes to His love. It was love that I needed. Love that healeth all our diseases. I thought I had found the Kingdom of Heaven, but I had yet to learn it was here in our midst—and all these things that I had been seeking should be added when I had found it. What I have gained myself I must share with others. The work is so big—the fields so wide—and the command is—"Go ye into all the world."

Yee Kui listened quietly—sucking his pipe. A faraway look was in his psychic eyes. As Arthur watched him he realized how invaluable his service had been—how invaluable it might still be on the great trip he had ahead. If he had only faith enough in the supply unfailing he would have taken him along—but he was still young—so very young in the practical belief, although so old in the study. He told him this—and the little Chinaman removed his pipe from his toothless mouth, and his smile made his yellow wrinkled face look beautiful.

"Where the master goes—I go, too," he said.

He went into his room as he spoke and brought out a bag which contained the savings of years—and a bank book.

"The master need me—I no need money—I go along —I help the master."

Then God had indeed provided for him—and here was the little Chinaman teaching him the great lesson in unfailing supply.

"But those are your savings, Yee Kui," he said. "What will you do when those have gone?"

"When those have gone!" he repeated. "When those have gone—then the good Lord send me more."

O, beautiful lesson in faith. It entered his heart and soul.

"Yes, the good Lord will send you more, Yee Kui," he answered. "Pressed down and running over shall be your share."

He walked away while he spoke. His heart was too full to say more. The words of gentle reproof seemed whispered in his soul.

"Wherefore didst thou doubt?"

Chapter XIX

UNTIL WE MEET AGAIN

Akana had returned. He was freed from all claim of leprosy, and radiant, bright and beautiful, he stood upon the shore holding the people spellbound by his story. They sat upon the sand, upon the rocks, they stood in their canoes and listened breathless while he talked. The blue sky melting into waters of deepest blue, the fronded palms, the fishers with their nets, the boats, the shore, how like the background that outlined the Teacher of two thousand years ago.

Beside her brother, Lilinoe was standing. She looked beautiful as she listened to his strong and sympathetic voice which held the audience by its tenderness and love. Joy was mingled with sadness in Arthur's heart as he gazed upon her. He tried to shut out by thoughts of service a sudden sense of his own loneliness.

At a little distance from the others, Ewaliko stood. His face was triumphant, and suddenly he pulled Lilinoe aside and eagerly began to talk.

"Lilinoe, I have seen Him," he whispered. "I have seen the One who has come to take you. Last night when I sat on the mountain He came to me. He reached out His shining hands, and the moon dropped all its light around Him and the stars fell over His head like a crown of gold. He is so beautiful I am willing that you should go with Him, for now I can never feel lonely, for wherever I look I can see His face. He comes into my music, and I shall play as I have never played before. He is going to take me up to heights that I have never trodden, where I can listen to songs of birds with mighty wings and sweetest voices—where I can look on flowers that live and give their scent forever—where there are no storms nor shipwrecks, and I shall never be afraid again. We are both going with Him, Lilinoe, but you go by a different bridge—all different ways, but all with Him. All meeting at the Rest House in the end.

He walked away while he was speaking, and began to ascend the mountain by another path from that which he hitherto had taken. The people turned, attracted by his music. Akana paused in speaking, and all in silence watched the ascending figure. Higher and higher he went, the notes of his music floating downward sweet as the scent of flowers upon the wind.

A silence still deeper fell over the watchers. The boy looked back a moment. His old fear of the heights had seized him. It was cold, so cold, the heavy mist surrounded him like snow banks; the landscape—all he loved below, had vanished. There was no way back, no calling to his people. He stood alone in the thick mist, no flower visible, no light, no song of bird. A wail of appeal went upwards from his soul. It was answered almost before it had found utterance—answered by the striking of a chord upon his fallen instrument—a chord so sweet so full of music, that like a sympathetic under-standing voice it broke all sense of loneliness.

The seeming snow banks melted round him—melted and took light airy forms of shining whiteness. Far below the watchers saw the clouds burst into one great brilliant flame. The Hawaiians seized each other's hands and fell upon their knees.

"He comes," they cried. "He comes, the One you told us of. He comes upon the heights!"

But the vision vanished quickly as it came. Only the few most spiritual had seen the face that Ewaliko saw.

The music that they heard was not played on earth's crude instruments, but instruments too fine for the human hands. Yet the listeners found themselves joining in that plaintive sound of greeting and farewell:

"Aloha oe, Aloha oe,
E ke onaona noho iki lipo,
A fond embrace, a hoi ae au,
Until we meet again."

"But when?" asked Iao, sadly, as he looked at Lilinoe. "When shall we meet again? It seems as if the parting of the ways has come for everyone of us."

"The voice is calling us where we are needed, Iao," she replied. "It is the road of service, but as Ewaliko said, it leads us all to the same Rest House in the end."

She closed her eyes in silence for a moment. Then in a sudden flash a picture rose before her, which made her face alive with joy. A picture maybe in the distant years —she was not given time. It gave her voice conviction as she answered:

"Yes, we shall all meet again. On this same ground we shall all meet. Beneath these sunny skies we shall embrace in our 'Aloha.' We shall all meet, for I have seen it—God's love is very great."

THE END

CPSIA information can be obtained
at www.ICGtesting.com
Printed in the USA
BVOW06s1938050617
486092BV00018B/254/P